My Million Dollar Investment Voyage

Retirement Saving Do's and Don'ts

2017 Edition

Author

Geezer Gammer

Published by 240CO LLC, Verdi, NV 89439

Edited By CreateSpace

ISBN-13: 978-0-9854231-4-8

ISBN-10: 0985423145

Publication Date: May 1, 2017

Library of Congress Control Number: 2017939368

Contents

Figures

Prologue

Q: Is there anything that you want to say to your readers, Mr. Gammer?

GG: Sure. Thanks for buying my book. I hope that you enjoy reading it and find that it helps you by learning about my investment strategies.

But please, just call me GG. I prefer not to be so formal.

Q: Okay, GG. Do you want to dedicate this book to anyone?

GG: Yes, my daughter.

Q: Why her?

GG: Because when I pass on, she will inherit my estate, and I want her to know how to handle it.

Q: Is there anyone you want to thank for helping you write this book?

GG: Yes. My sister Susan, her husband Milton, my sister Barbara, and my friends John, Victor, Tyrell, Carole and David. They all read my proof copies and made some excellent recommendations for improvements.

Q: Is there anything else that you want your readers to know?

GG: Yes. Everything that I am going to talk about actually happened during my life.

Q: So this is a true story?

GG: Yes. The investment strategies that I eventually found to work for me were distilled from my own successes and failures.

Introduction

Q: How old are you?

GG: I was born in 1941 and it's now 2017, so that makes me seventy-six years old.

By the way, in case you're a history buff, Hitler commemorated my birth by sending millions of German troops into Russia two days later.

Q: Well, you definitely are an old geezer. I'm not a history buff, but I'm sure glad that I wasn't living in Russia in 1941.

Qualifications

Q: What qualifies you to write about investing?

GG: Well, I have over a million dollars in my retirement accounts.

Q: I'm impressed. How many years have you been investing?

GG: Fifty, and I've been through lots of market booms and busts.

Q: Did you do the investing on your own or did you have advisers?

GG: Both, but most of the time I've done it by myself.

Types of Investments

Q: Just what do you consider to be an investment?

GG: Something that you buy that will appreciate or generate income.

Q: So what did you invest in?

GG: Lots of different stuff over the years: life insurance, houses, stocks, bonds, options, gold mines, and oil wells.

Q: Which were the worst ones?

GG: The gold mines and oil wells.

I got audited on my tax deductions for the gold mines and that taught me never to tangle with the IRS again.

And, as you can probably guess, the oil wells all dried up. So after those experiences, I avoided the complicated stuff, and I stuck with simpler investments.

Q: What are options?

GG: Bets that you make on stuff going up or down.

Getting the Money to Invest

But before we start talking about them we should talk about getting enough money to start investing with.

Q: All right. How can you get a lot of money fast?

GG: You can rob a bank, but you better watch *Butch Cassidy and the Sundance Kid* first. It's a great movie.

Q: Quit kidding around.

GG: Well, you could win the lottery, but your chances are pretty slim.

Q: Get serious!

GG: Okay. You could inherit it, just like my daughter is going to do.

Q: How did you get your money?

GG: I inherited some from my father, but most of it I earned.

Q: How did you earn it?

GG: I worked for some big corporations.

Q: How many?

GG: Four.

Q: Which ones?

GG: The first one was a computer manufacturer, the second built steel and chemical plants, the third was a computer timesharing company and the last one manufactured drugs and cosmetics.

Q: That's quite a few. Why did you change jobs so many times?

GG: Well, I left the first one to double my salary at the second one. After that I had to change jobs because fate intervened.

Q: What do you mean?

GG: Well, the second one was destroyed by a greedy financier, and the third one failed.

Q: How long were you at the drug and cosmetics company?

GG: Sixteen years.

Q: What did you do there?

GG: For most of the time, I was responsible for their international computer systems.

Q: Did you retire from that company?

GG: Nope, I quit to start a small one of my own.

Q: Why?

GG: Because that company got emasculated by another greedy financier.

Q: What did your own company do?

GG: Developed computer software.

Q: Did you create some cool software and sell out to a big company for millions?

GG: Nope. I created custom systems for large corporations that retained all the rights to them.

Q: How many years did you do that for?

GG: For twenty-seven years until I was seventy years old and shut the company down.

But we are going a bit off track here. We're supposed to be talking about getting money to invest with, not my work history.

Q: Okay, so how did you get your investing money?

GG: By following a simple formula.

Q: What was it?

GG: I spent less than I earned and saved the rest.

Q: Duh! Everybody knows that.

GG: Yeah, but not everybody does it.

Q: Well, you're certainly right about that. So what's your secret?

GG: First, I got the best education that I could afford. I went to Penn State University, worked part-time jobs while attending college, and worked summers to help out my father who was footing the cost of my education. I graduated in 1963.

Q: So education came first. What came second?

GG: Hard work. When I was getting started, I had two jobs for many years.

Managing Expenses

Q: I'm guessing that the next thing you did was to limit your spending.

GG: You bet. In a consumer economy like ours, there are a vast number of goods and services available. But only some are really essential, and I tried to focus my spending on those first.

Q: What are they?

GG: Well, as you might expect, food, clothing, and shelter led the list. I also needed a car because I wasn't living in a big city with good mass transit.

Q: What did you avoid spending on?

GG: Expensive cars. They just didn't make sense to me. I never thought that their gadgetry and fancy furnishings were worth their premium prices. Anyway, their best features eventually migrate down to the less expensive lower-status cars.

But less expensive cars don't have to be boring. I once even owned a sports car. Would you like to see a picture of it?

Q: Sure.

FIGURE 1 1974 SAAB SONNET III

Pretty cool, huh? It's a Saab Sonnet III that I bought in 1974. It had a fiberglass body and got over 30 mpg from its 96 horsepower V4 engine. That was really great during the energy crisis of the 1970s, when you had to line up for hours at a station to get gas.

I kept it until 1987 and gave it to my teenage son, who spent a year fixing it up. Alas, it was destroyed in a foggy multicar pileup, but fortunately he was uninjured.

Q: So you kept the car for thirteen years—that's a long time. How long do you typically keep a car?

GG: In the old days, I kept them until they wore out. But now that the cars have become so computerized and complex to maintain, I keep them only until their extended warranties expire.

Q: Clearly you aren't a big spender on cars. What else did you save money on?

GG: I tried to minimize credit-card debt as much as possible. The card interest rates have always been very high, and it didn't make sense to use them unless I was really in a financial jam.

Q: So how much did you tuck away before you started investing?

GG: A year's worth of living expenses.

Q: Where did you keep the money?

GG: In a bank.

Q: Why?

GG: Because it was safe. If the bank failed, the government guaranteed that I wouldn't lose it.

Q: You weren't exactly a big risk-taker, were you?

GG: Nope. I certainly wasn't when I first started to earn a living.

Taking Risks

Q: Well, to make a million bucks for your retirement I'm betting that you had to take some risks. Did you?

GG: Yep. And I'm still taking them.

Q: Why?

GG: I had to learn to accept risk because if I didn't I couldn't earn enough on my investment money to stay ahead of inflation.

Q: So what did you invest in?

GG: Insurance, houses, stocks, and bonds—but I used to invest in options as well.

Q: What are options?

GG: Bets that you make on stuff going up or down.

Q: How did you do with those?

GG: Not too well. You have to guess what the future is going to be like, and I've never been very good at that.

Q: Did the bonds work out for you?

GG: Some did and some didn't. When I was earning money, the nontaxable income from municipal bonds was good to have. I bought the lower-quality ones because they paid a higher interest rate. Some bond-funded projects went bust and their bonds became worthless, but most were okay.

Q: Did you ever invest in commodity futures?

GG: Nope. They are just like betting on options, and I just can't see into the future well enough to gamble with them.

Q: How about junk bonds?

GG: I bought some of those, but for the same risk level, I was able to do better with dividend-paying stocks.

Q: What did you invest in first?

Insurance

Whole-Life Policy

GG: In 1962, at my father's urging, I bought my first life insurance policy. It was a whole-life policy that would pay $5,000 to my heirs when I died, as long as I paid the quarterly premiums of $30.22 on time. I also chose to invest the policy dividends in additional paid-up insurance.

At that time $5,000 was a lot of money. The average income per year was $6,450, and the average cost of a new car was $2,650.

Q: Did that turn out to be a good investment?

GG: Not at all. As of 2015 the policy, including the additional paid up insurance, was worth $8,344. The cash surrender value of the policy was $6,502.

Q: So why wasn't it a good investment?

GG: Because of inflation: in 2015, the average American earned $55,775, and the average new car cost $33,560.

Looking at it another way, the total of inflation-adjusted premiums that I invested in this policy over fifty-four years was $19,537. So if I had invested my premiums at an annual rate of return equal to inflation, I would have $11,193 more than the policy will pay when I die.

Q: But you had the insurance coverage and the peace of mind that brought you.

GG: You are right, of course, but there is a much less expensive way to insure your life.

Q: What is it?

Term-Life Policy

GG: Term-life insurance: instead of the insurance company guaranteeing your life forever, they do it for a limited number of years. They have longevity on their side.

Q: How is that?

GG: Look at this chart.

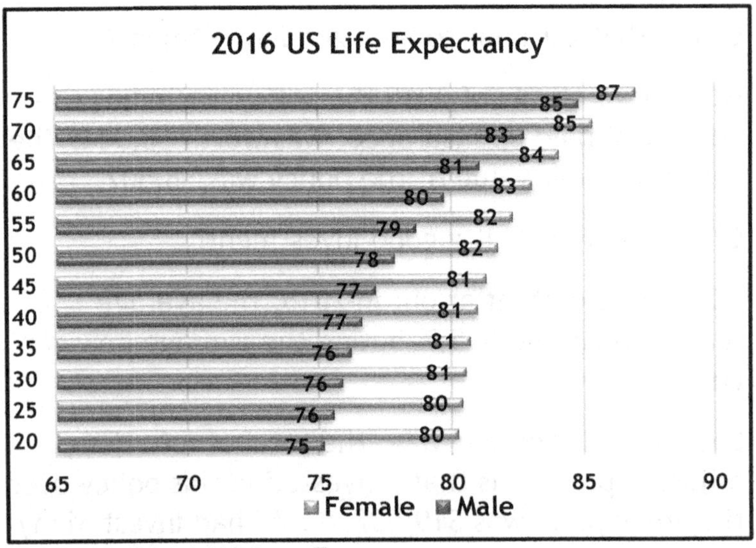

FIGURE 2 2016 US LIFE EXPECTANCY

Q: What does it show?

GG: How long you will live based upon your age in 2016; as you can see, the ladies are on top. They live longer than men—but almost everyone will live to be seventy-five.

Q: I think I understand. The insurance company doesn't have to pay off term policies very often—so that keeps the premiums a lot lower.

GG: Right.

You will probably only need life insurance for those years when you have large debts—like a house mortgage. So it's not necessary to pay for it into your old age.

Comparing the Two

Let's see how different the numbers would be if I had purchased term insurance. The median price of a house in the United States in 1963 was $17,200. Let's say that back then, I took a conventional thirty-year mortgage with 20 percent down and financed the rest.

If I wanted to make sure the mortgage was paid off when the grim reaper got me, I would need a term-life policy for $13,760 for thirty years. Let's say that I decided to cover my funeral expenses too and bought $14,000 of coverage beginning in 1963 when I was twenty-two years old.

Q: This should be interesting.

GG: It turns out that the annual premium for $14,000 of the thirty-year term insurance would have been $17 dollars versus $121 for the $5,000 whole-life policy.

Q: That's a huge difference!

GG: Yes, and when you do the adjustments for inflation it turns out that if I had invested the difference between the cost of the whole-life and term policies at an annual rate of return equal to inflation, my total investment after fifty-four years would be worth $17,247.

That's twice as much as the $8,334 that the whole-life policy is worth. In addition, I would have had more than enough money to pay off the mortgage because the principal would have decreased each year.

Staying Insured

Q: So if your whole-life policy is such a bad investment, why do you keep it?

GG: That's a good question. There are two answers.

First, the policy's cash surrender value is $6,502 and that is considerably less than the $8,344 death benefit. In addition, if my demise is due to an accident, the policy pays an additional $5,000. So for an annual expense of $121, it isn't worth canceling.

Q: That makes sense. What's the second answer?

GG: I had a lot of health issues over the years, and it was impossible for me to get term insurance.

Q: I'm sorry to hear that.

GG: Well, I'm still here thanks to modern medicine. However, as you can see, it's a good idea to buy your term insurance when you are young. The rates are the lowest then, and you are in your physical prime of life so you probably won't be refused coverage.

Q: So if insurance was your first investment, what did you invest in next?

Housing

My First House

GG: Well, in 1968, five years after I finished college, I bought my first house.

Q: Is housing a good investment?

GG: Yes—if you follow the 20/25 rule. Once you have saved enough for a 20 percent down payment and have reached at least the 25 percent income tax bracket it's a no-brainer.

Q: Why do you say that?

GG: Well, you have to live somewhere and paying rent doesn't accumulate anything for you. Rent also increases over time due to inflation whereas a fixed-rate mortgage payment remains constant.

You can also deduct your mortgage interest on your income taxes so you end up reducing your shelter expenses by the same percentage as the tax bracket that you are in.

Q: How about an example of how that works?

GG: Okay. Suppose that you are in the 25 percent income tax bracket. Twenty-five cents of every dollar that you earn goes to the federal government to keep our country going.

If you pay $10,000 annually in mortgage interest, you save $2,500 in taxes. That effectively reduces your mortgage expense to $7,500—so you have lowered your shelter expenses by 25 percent and that's the same as your tax bracket.

In addition, you can deduct your house real-estate taxes and that adds even more to the financial benefits of owning your own home.

The Great Recession

Q: Okay, I get it. But I don't understand why you say it's a no-brainer. How about the millions of people who lost their homes during the Great Recession?

GG: Well, my daughter was one of them. She lost everything, and her credit was ruined.

Q: So how can housing be a good investment?

GG: The Great Recession problems didn't arise from investing in houses. The problems resulted from bad lending practices and the failure to build up home equity.

Q: What do you mean?

GG: Let's take my daughter's case. She started prudently enough following the 20/25 rule.

But adjustable rate mortgages with low initial teaser rates became readily available. It became a common practice to refinance your home and use the extracted equity to buy anything that you wanted.

So she did what millions of others did: refinanced her mortgage and then used the 20 percent down payment that she pulled out of her home equity to buy an expensive truck.

Of course, just like so many others caught in this financial trap, she couldn't afford the monthly payments once the teaser rate expired and the extremely high mortgage rate kicked in.

She couldn't refinance because housing prices were falling, and she owed more than the house was worth. So she lost her house and her life savings.

Q: After that sad tale I repeat my question—how can housing be a good investment?

The Long-Term View

GG: During the Great Recession, millions and millions of people kept their houses and continued to enjoy the benefits of homeownership because they viewed their house as a long-term investment.

Here's a graph that shows what I mean.

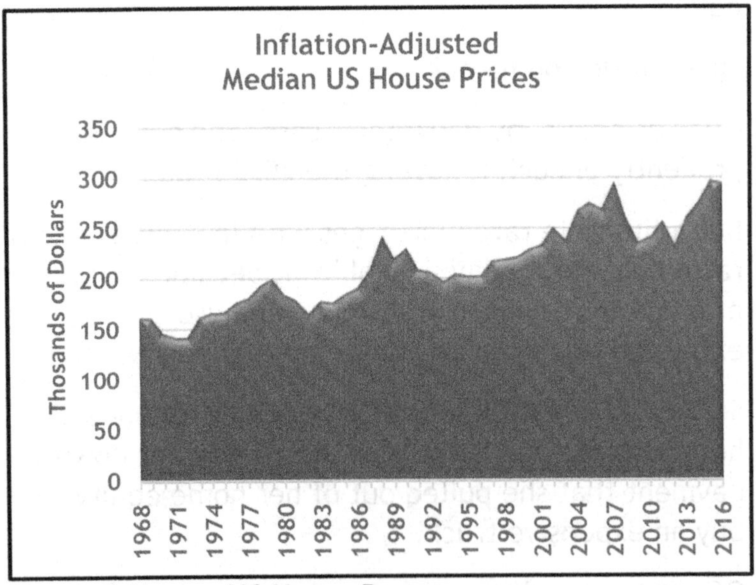

FIGURE 3 MEDIAN US HOUSE PRICES

Q: So what does it show?

GG: A couple of things. First, over a forty-eight-year-period house prices increased an average of 5.6 percent a year, and second, it shows that house prices can change a lot from year to year.

Q: So if you bought when prices were high and sold when prices were low, you would lose money.

GG: Of course. But a house is a rather unique investment because you are living in it. Unless something drastic happens that prevents you from being able to pay the mortgage, you don't have to sell it when prices are low.

Q: So you feel richer when your house is more valuable and poorer when it's less valuable, but it really does increase in value over the long term.

GG: Exactly, but you need to be patient. It took nine years for houses to regain the value that they lost in the Great Recession.

But there's another advantage to owning your home.

Q: What is it?

Trading Up

GG: Once your equity builds up, you can reinvest it in a different house and I did that several times.

Q: Tell me about it.

GG: Well, my house purchases were pretty typical for an American dad with a couple of kids. I kept the first one that I told you about earlier for two years.

With the children growing up, I bought a larger one that had a bigger yard and was in a really good neighborhood with excellent schools. I kept that one for eight years.

I ended up with half of that house's equity in a divorce settlement and then, like a lot of other divorcees, I rented for a few years to recover from the emotional and financial trauma.

Q: I'm sorry to hear that. What did you do next?

GG: I bought a four-story town house designed so that the first floor could be rented as an apartment. I kept that one for fifteen years and lived there with my second wife.

Q: It sounds like a pretty practical setup. What came next?

GG: After the kids graduated from college, my new wife and I bought an empty-nester home and renovated it into our dream house.

Q: Sounds neat.

GG: It was. But as I neared retirement age, I needed a less expensive one so I sold it after four years and bought a smaller one. We lived together in that house for thirteen years.

Q: Where do you live now?

GG: In a small but very comfortable home in a nice retirement community.

Q: So you basically parlayed the equity from one house into another—is that right?

GG: Yes, and I eventually extracted some of the accumulated house equity when I downsized the last two houses. That money has really come in handy during retirement.

Special Concerns

However, there are several things that I learned to be concerned about when I invested in housing.

Q: What are they?

GG: First, unlike stocks and bonds, houses require maintenance and that can cost a lot of money. You have to be financially prepared for things like new water heaters, plumbing fixtures, central air compressors, reroofing, and repainting. The maintenance of the landscaping and the HVAC systems also need to be planned for.

Second, a house is an illiquid investment. It takes time to sell it, the brokerage fees are high, and they are usually paid by the seller.

Third, in order to increase the value of your house, you need to buy in the best neighborhood that you can afford.

Of the five houses that I bought and sold, only the townhouse was located in a marginal neighborhood, and I sold it for exactly the same price that I bought it for. I consoled myself by figuring out that I had lived there rent-free through the years because my tax savings covered the maintenance costs.

I made some really good lifelong friends in that neighborhood and that partially compensated for the fact that had I invested in a better location the house value would have doubled in fifteen years.

Fourth, you have to avoid buying a home that is too expensive. Make sure that you can meet the mortgage payments without overstretching your budget.

In the excitement of shopping for a house, it's easy to forget all the other expenses that you may face. For example, here is a list of some essential ones.

Food	At home, fast food
Clothing	For home and work
Transportation	Cars, trucks, fuel, maintenance, work commute
Insurance	Health, vehicle, home
Communications	Phone, TV, internet
Education	Yours and your offspring's
Children	Multiply everything above by the number of your kids
Retirement	To retire at age sixty-seven, you need eight to twenty years of income

Figure 4 Essential Living Expenses

As if that's not enough to think about, here are just a few of the optional ways to spend your money.

Recreation	Sports, travel, gym
Entertainment	Restaurants, theatre, movies, plays, concerts

Personal	Babysitting, hair, nails, spa
Merchandise	High fashion, jewelry, electronics
Pets	Dogs, cats, birds, fish, horses
Weddings	For your daughter(s) and attending those of others
Hobbies	Photography, cooking, music, video gaming
RVs	Boats, motorcycles, campers, off-road vehicles
Insurance	Life, liability, pet, RV

Figure 5 Optional Living Expenses

Fifth, if you choose to move to a new house, the stress and expense of changing locations is considerable.

Finally, it's natural to want a beautiful home and that's one of the advantages that a house provides over a rented apartment—you can improve it to your heart's content. But if you overdo it, you'll have a difficult time recovering the money that you have poured into it. That's what happened with our dream house.

Q: Thanks for the warnings. Now that I'm aware of all this I understand why you are a housing advocate. But if it's good to own one home, what about investing in a second home?

Buying a Second Home

GG: Well, the same income tax savings are available for interest payments on a second home, but there are some things that you need to be aware of.

Q: What are they?

GG: If you use it only yourself, or rent it out for fourteen or fewer days (which by the way isn't taxed), the mortgage interest and real-estate taxes are fully deductible—as long as the total of your primary and second home mortgages is less than $1.1 million.

If you rent it out for more than fourteen days, you need to report all your rental income. You can deduct the house expenses from the rental income, and they are prorated according to the number of rental days divided by the total days the house is used.

As long as the expenses, including depreciation, mortgage interest, property taxes, insurance premiums, property manager costs, and utilities don't exceed your rental income you can deduct them all.

Q: What happens if you have a loss?

GG: It gets complicated. If you limit your personal use to fourteen days or less, then you might be able to deduct up to $25,000 of losses if your annual income is less than a certain threshold, currently set at $100,000.

Q: So did you invest in a second home?

GG: Over the years my second wife and I bought two timeshares as second homes. The first one worked out but the second was a disaster.

Q: What happened?

GG: The first one was at the Disney Vacation Club at Walt Disney World in Orlando. It was purchased in 1993, and we sold it twenty years later for the same amount that we paid for it.

Q: Earlier you pointed out that this kind of investment is only break-even when you ignore inflation.

GG: That's true, but our vacation costs were reduced by our tax bracket percentage of the mortgage and real-estate taxes. And there were other benefits too.

In addition to enjoying taking our children, grandchildren and other family members there, we were able to exchange our unit for some great stays at other hotels and resorts.

Once the kids were on their way, we occasionally rented it out. And because it was rented for less than fourteen days, the income wasn't taxed. Also by then the rent was considerably more than the annual expenses and mortgage payment.

Q: It sounds like a fun investment even if it didn't really increase in value over the years. What happened with the other timeshare?

GG: We were staying on the Hawaiian Island of Kauai at a resort that we exchanged for our Disney timeshare.

We fell in love with the island's beauty and its peaceful ambience. There were far fewer tourists in Kauai than on the more popular Hawaiian Islands that we had visited previously.

We mistakenly allowed ourselves to be lured into attending a high-pressure sales presentation while there and were talked into buying a second timeshare.

Q: What went wrong?

GG: We bought it expecting to stay there during the winter months when it was cold on the mainland. But whenever we tried to book a date, all the winter months were always already taken, so the whole point of having the place was meaningless.

Q: So what did you do?

GG: After two frustrating years of paying increasingly higher maintenance fees, I paid off the mortgage and handed the property back to the timeshare company.

We lost everything that we had invested just to get rid of the maintenance fees because we couldn't use the place when we wanted to. And it became clear that the fees would keep going up year after year.

Q: Ouch!

GG: Yes, the lesson that we learned from that experience was to avoid high-pressure sales pitches.

Rental Property

Q: Did you ever invest in a property to rent?

GG: Yes, in a manner of speaking.

Q: What do you mean?

GG: Well, the townhouse that I owned was constructed so that the first floor was a one-bedroom apartment, and we lived above it on the second and third floors. I rented out the apartment and used the income to help pay for our housing expenses.

The first tenants were a young couple who had a cat that apparently disliked his litter box. After they moved out, I had to replace part of the urine-soaked floor and all the carpet as well as the thoroughly clawed window screens. The place also required repainting throughout.

The second tenant was a retired schoolteacher who sold her home and was seeking a quiet apartment. Unfortunately, with us living on the floors above her, the apartment didn't meet her standards for silence. She complained constantly, and I finally let her out of the lease just to get some peace of mind.

Because of these experiences, I learned that I didn't have the temperament to be a landlord, but I eventually found a tenant that I could deal with.

Q: Who was it?

GG: Me.

I converted the apartment into an office, rented it to myself, and set up my software development company there. I had a very short commute to work and loved it.

Q: Clever.

Q: Okay, we've pretty much covered housing. So what else did you invest in?

Saving for Retirement

How Much to Save

GG: I made it a point to save the maximum amount that I could for retirement by using the government's approved retirement plans.

Social security is mandatory, so that was a nonchoice.

Next came my employers' pension plans. When they were supplemented by 401(k) plans I invested in them too.

When I left the corporate world, I moved my 401(k) assets into an individual IRA.

I invested in a SEP IRA while I was self-employed and then when my tax bracket was lower, I moved some assets into a Roth IRA.

Q: That all sounds quite prudent but it seems complex too.

GG: In order to provide for your retirement adequately, you need to deal with the complexity whether you like it or not—because the longer you live, the longer you can expect to live. Here's a chart that shows what I mean.

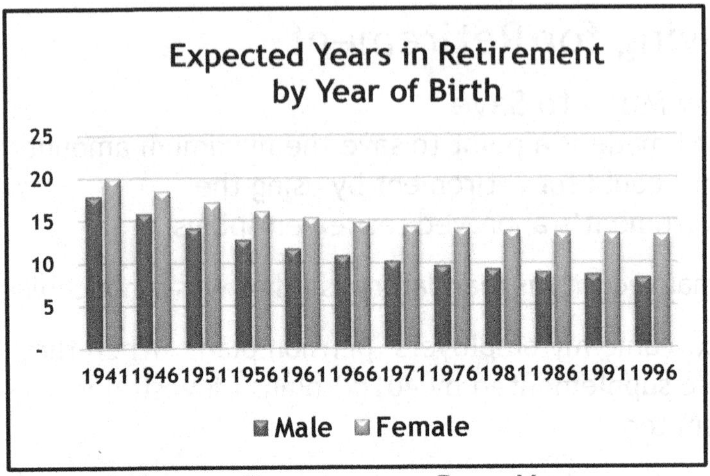

FIGURE 6 YEARS IN RETIREMENT BY BIRTH YEAR

Assuming that men retire at sixty-seven they will need retirement income that lasts for eight to eighteen years. Women have a bigger challenge because they live longer, so if they retire at sixty-seven they will need their income to last for thirteen to twenty years. These figures are based upon 2016 life expectancies.

Q: Those are long times for sure. So what are all these different plans that you invested in?

Social Security

GG: I've always viewed social security as my charitable contribution to the less fortunate in the country.

The program was implemented during the Great Depression to provide a financial safety net for saving the elderly from being destitute. I believe that it meets this very commendable social goal and that the program should never be stopped.

However, as an investment, viewed purely in financial terms, it's not so great. When I run the inflation-adjusted numbers, they show that if I had invested the amount that I contributed throughout the years it would provide the same annual payment that I now receive—but I would still have the capital. Social security pays me only while I'm alive, and there isn't any capital left when I'm gone.

There is only one decision that you can make with this mandatory program and that is when to start drawing your retirement payments out.

If you were born after 1960, sixty-seven is the full retirement age to start receiving the so-called "benefits" that you were required to pay for during your entire working life. If you were born before 1960 that age depends upon your birth year. I was born in 1941, so my full retirement age was sixty-five years and eight months.

You can choose early retirement beginning at age sixty-two but that can reduce your payments by up to 30 percent—and that's a lot. You can also delay receiving benefits until age seventy and that will increase them by 7 percent a year for each year that you delay beyond your normal benefit age.

The decision that you make depends upon how much you need the money to live on in retirement and how many years that you think you will be alive.

In my case I could afford to wait until I was sixty-five. But my longevity genes aren't great, and I've had some serious health issues over the years, so I didn't want to gamble on starting at seventy. After mulling it over for a while I finally decided to start receiving payments at sixty-five.

Only time will tell if I made the right decision to start at that age. If I live to be eighty-two, I will have received cumulative payments equal to those that I made over my lifetime. If I make it to my expected life-span of eight-six years, then I will have beaten the system—assuming that the program doesn't go broke before then.

Pension

GG: Speaking of going broke, let's talk next about my pension.

Q: I'm guessing that you have experienced some pension problems.

GG: Yes, and that's why I decided not to depend solely upon a pension for funding my retirement.

Do you remember when I told you about the cosmetics and drug company that I worked at for seventeen years?

Q: The one that got emasculated by a greedy financier?

GG: That's the one. In his heartless quest to amass a huge private fortune, he gutted the retirement fund and left those of us who had spent our lives building the company holding a nearly empty bag.

I was pretty sure that I wasn't going to get anything, but the Pension Benefit Guarantee Corporation stepped in and helped to supplement the small portion that he hadn't stolen.

I figured that the company would eventually go bankrupt, so I chose to take my pension as soon as I could and that turned out to be at age sixty.

Because I took it early I received a relatively small payment, but at least I got something for all my years of work.

However, I did manage to extract a small measure of revenge.

Q: How did you do that?

GG: My second wife was twelve years younger than me, so I chose to take the pension payments structured for married couples with a 50 percent survivorship payment to my wife when I passed away. Being forty-eight, with an expected life-span of eighty-three, she would be receiving money from that company for a long, long time, provided it didn't file for bankruptcy.

But it still galls me mightily when I get my monthly pension payment to see that the company, whose decimated remnants have somehow managed to still struggle on, is responsible for only 16 percent of it while the government has to foot the bill for the remaining 84 percent.

Q: I can certainly understand that. With all the mergers, buyouts, corporate bankruptcies, and financially strapped unions as well as underfunded state and local government pensions, I'm sure that it must have happened to millions of people.

GG: It certainly has. But not all pensions end up badly. My wife was fortunate enough to work for a reputable, well-run company and accumulated a nice pension there.

Q: Did she choose to take monthly payments when she retired?

GG: No, her health wasn't good, so she decided that taking a lump-sum distribution would be better. She rolled it into an IRA to avoid paying income taxes until she needed to withdraw money from the IRA account.

Had she chosen to take monthly payments, they would have stopped if she passed away. By taking the lump sum she ensured that she retained the full value of everything that she had accrued.

Q: Okay. So after these pension experiences you decided that other investments would be necessary to provide for your retirement. What did you invest in next?

401(k) Plan

GG: In the 1980s, 401(k) plans became available at many large corporations including the ones that my wife and I worked at. These plans allowed us to contribute a portion of our earnings into them before the income tax deductions were made.

In addition, our employers made matching contributions as a percentage of what we put in.

Each annual matching contribution was vested over a several-year period as an inducement not to change jobs.

The assets in these plans, including their earnings such as interest, dividends, and capital gains accumulate without being taxed. Withdrawals can begin without penalty starting at age 59½. When they are eventually taken, they're taxed as ordinary income.

The choice of what to invest your 401(k) contributions in are limited to those offered by the corporation. In both plans the company's common stock was available.

Q: How much did you contribute into these plans?

GG: The maximum amount possible because the matching contributions seemed to be pure investment gravy. But not everything worked out as we had expected.

Q: What happened?

GG: In both plans we chose to invest part of our savings in the company's stock and the matching contributions were in company stock too. When we eventually rolled the 401(k) assets into our IRA accounts the value of the company stock was less than we had invested in it.

Q: Bummer.

GG: Yes, it was a mistake to rely on the company too much. But the other assets that we selected grew nicely, so all in all we did okay.

Q: You mentioned rolling into your IRA accounts. How does that work?

Individual IRA

GG: IRA accounts are my favorite retirement savings vehicle because you can choose from a vast array things to invest in.

As with the 401(k) plan, the assets in an IRA plan, including their earnings such as interest, dividends, and capital gains accumulate without being taxed. Withdrawals without penalty also cannot begin before you reach 59½ and when they are taken they're taxed as ordinary income as well.

But to answer your question, to roll over you provide the 401(k) plan administrators with the details of your IRA account, and they do a nontaxable transfer within sixty days after your departure from the company.

Q: That's certainly easy enough. But, other than rolling over your 401(k), how do you add money into an IRA account?

GG: You need to be earning income and be under 70½. Then you are allowed to contribute a maximum amount each year and deduct it from your taxable earnings.

The maximum contributable amount is currently $5,500 or the amount of your taxable earnings, whichever is smaller. If you are over fifty, then you can contribute an additional $1,000 for a total of $6,500.

Q: Can you contribute to a 401(k) plan and an IRA too?

GG: Yes. You can contribute up to the maximum amount allowed into each as long as your taxable income is less than a certain amount.

The limit is currently set at $61,000 for a single person and there are different limits for married folks. Above these limits, the maximum deduction is reduced and eventually reaches zero.

SEP IRA

Q: What type of retirement plan did you have when you were self-employed?

GG: It was a Simplified Employee Pension or SEP plan. I was able to put up to 25 percent of my own and also up to 25 percent of my employees' income into a separate account for each of us annually.

There was a maximum amount that could be contributed and that changed over the years but is currently set at $54,000 and that seems adequate to me.

There were a couple of special considerations for the SEP IRA accounts. The contribution percentage had to be the same for everyone and only the employer could contribute. That meant that the employees couldn't contribute any additional money.

Q: You certainly did have a lot of retirement accounts. Were there any others?

Roth IRA

GG: Yes, I also invested in a Roth IRA.

Q: What's that?

GG: An account that you contribute to but can't deduct the amount from your taxable income. However, the withdrawals are tax free, including those resulting from the assets that you invested in.

Q: It doesn't sound like there's much benefit from doing that.

GG: Well, it's not as beneficial as an individual IRA, but here's how I was able to use one to shield earnings.

After I passed sixty, in the years that I was still earning money, but below the government limits prohibiting it, I rolled assets from my Individual IRA into a Roth IRA.

I had to pay taxes on the Individual IRA withdrawals but once the money was in the Roth account, as long as the account was open for at least five years, no taxes were due on any money that I withdrew from it.

And the biggest benefit was that I didn't have to take money from it once I reached 70½.

RMD

Q: Are you telling me that the government can force you to withdraw money from your retirement accounts?

GG: You bet. Remember that you haven't paid any income taxes on the contributions made into your IRAs, so the IRS forces you to withdraw money when you reach 70½.

It is called a required minimum distribution, and you pay the long-deferred taxes on the amount you withdraw according to the tax bracket that you are in at the time you take the money out.

Q: How much do you have to withdraw?

GG: They use a table of numbers that decrease as your age increases. You divide your previous year-end IRA value by the number assigned to your age.

Q: So you have to withdraw more each year?

GG: Yes, because the numbers keep getting smaller. But the IRA never becomes completely depleted while you are living.

IRA Inheritance

Q: So what happens to the money in it when you finally kick the bucket?

GG: It goes to the person you designated in your IRA account. If your spouse is the recipient and has an IRA, the deceased spouse's IRA gets rolled into it without being taxed.

If the surviving spouse is under 70½ then no further RMDs are required. However, when he or she reaches the RMD age the whole process starts over again.

Q: What if the recipient isn't a spouse?

GG: It gets more complex. But the wisest strategy for the recipient is to restart the RMD process using a table based upon the recipient's age. That way he or she will have income from the IRA for the rest of their lives.

Working in Retirement

Q: Well, you've certainly been a retirement savings champion but what happens if someone doesn't have enough money saved up for retirement?

GG: Then they are going to have to work. Take a look at this chart.

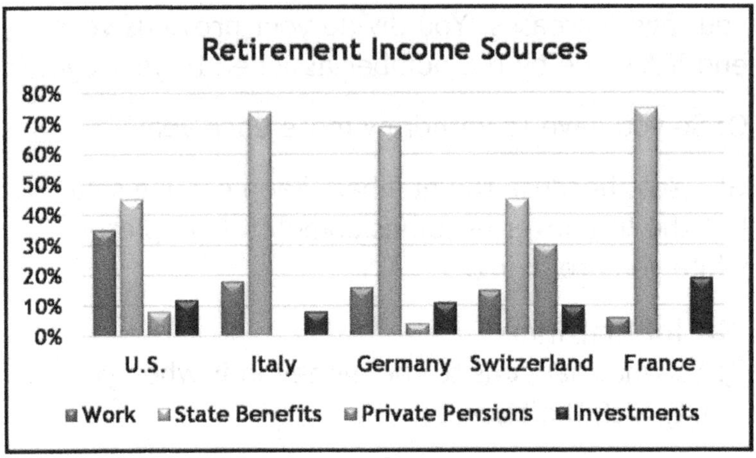

FIGURE 7 RETIREMENT INCOME SOURCES

The vertical bars are in the order shown on the bottom of the chart.

They show that Americans get 35 percent of their retirement income from working. The next closest country is Italy where very few have private pensions so the retirees must earn 18 percent.

Q: It appears that our social security system doesn't provide nearly as much income to retire on as the systems in the other countries do.

GG: Yes. Except for Switzerland, which provides the same 45 percent; however, the Swiss receive 30 percent from private pensions versus only 8 percent in the United States. That's why it's so important to set savings aside to retire on.

Q: Okay, I'm convinced. If you want to have a comfortable life when you retire, then you've got to save for it.

Q: So how did you invest your savings?

Growing Financial Assets

GG: There are three ways to increase your financial assets. You can accrue interest, collect dividends, and make capital gains.

Q: Which did you choose?

GG: All three.

Interest

GG: Lending money at interest is considered by many to be the least risky type of financial investment. Over the years, I bought bank CDs, bonds, and money-market funds in order to generate interest income.

Bank CDs are the least liquid. The bank agrees to pay you a fixed interest rate for a certain time period and then returns your capital along with the interest.

Bonds are legal agreements to pay a fixed interest rate for a specified time period after which the principal is returned to the lender. Their value fluctuates as their coupon interest rate rises above or falls below the prevailing market rate.

Their safety and interest rate depend upon the creditworthiness of the borrower. The safest, thus the ones paying the lowest interest rate, are those of the US government. The riskiest are the junk bonds issued by highly indebted corporations or big-spending governments and these pay the highest interest rates.

Money-market funds hold very short-term loans called commercial paper. They are managed in a manner that preserves the capital invested in them. They are priced at one dollar per share and are easily bought and sold. They are quite safe and consequently pay a low interest rate.

Dividends

Q: What are dividends?

GG: Dividends are profits distributed by corporations to their stockholders.

Profits are equal to the total sales of the company after subtracting all the expenses required to generate them.

Corporations can decide how much of their profits to distribute to their shareholders. Those that are growing rapidly normally reinvest their profits in their business and usually don't pay any dividends. More mature companies pay varying amounts of their profits to their shareholders.

Dividends are usually paid quarterly and are determined by dividing the amount of profit to be distributed by the total number of shares of stock that the all the stockholders own at that time.

Corporations that pay dividends often try to increase the amount that they return to their stockholders each year. This increasing revenue stream helps to increase their stock value.

There is no legal requirement for corporations to pay dividends. If business conditions deteriorate or the company's management makes bad decisions, the dividends are often reduced or completely eliminated.

Capital Gains

Q: What are capital gains?

GG: Capital gains result when you sell an asset that you bought for more than you paid for it.

If the asset is held in an IRA account, the gains aren't taxed. If it's held in a non-IRA account, it is taxed based upon when the sale is made.

Q: How does that work?

GG: If you held the asset for a year or less it's called a short-term gain and the tax rate is the same as that for your other income. If you held the asset for more than a year it becomes a long-term gain and the tax rates are lower.

Q: What happens if you sell the asset for less than you paid for it?

GG: If it's in an IRA account, the total value of your assets decreases by the amount of the loss.

If it's in a non-IRA account, you also suffer the loss of capital of course, but you can subtract all your capital losses from all your capital gains and then pay the tax on the difference thus reducing the taxes on your gains.

If your total losses exceed your total gains, then up to $3,000 can be deducted from your taxable income in that year. If you lose more than $3,000, the losses beyond that can be used to reduce your taxable income in subsequent years.

Investing in Securities

Q: How did you decide what to invest in?

The Market RR Car

GG: Before I answer that question it's important to tell you about my view of the financial markets.

Q: Okay.

GG: You really have to understand this because it helps you deal with the stress of investing.

Q: I'll pay close attention.

GG: You know that in the world of finance an investor who is optimistic that the markets will increase in value is called a bull.

Q: Sure, everyone knows that, and a pessimistic investor who thinks the markets will decrease in value is called a bear.

GG: Right. Now try to create this mental picture.

Imagine a railroad track that runs through a rainforest and emerges into a desert. There's a single open-top gondola car on the track and it is located half in the rainforest and half in the desert.

Q: Got it. Now what?

GG: The amount of water in the car represents the total value of all the investments in the markets—trillions and trillions of dollars.

There are a bunch of bears in the rainforest pushing on their end of the car and a bunch of bulls in the desert pushing on the other end.

Q: I think I see where you are going with this.

GG: Right. When there are more bulls than bears, the car gets pushed into the rainforest and fills up with more water. This represents the markets going up.

Q: And I'll bet that when there are more bears than bulls, the car gets pushed into the desert and the water evaporates, pushing the markets down.

GG: Correct. When the car is in the rainforest for a long time it's called a bull market, and when it's in the desert for a long time it's called a bear market.

Q: Okay, I get the picture, so what's the big deal?

GG: Over a long period of time, the Market RR Car has always filled up more in a bull market than it did in the previous bull market.

Q: Are you sure?

GG: Absolutely. Here's a graph that shows it...

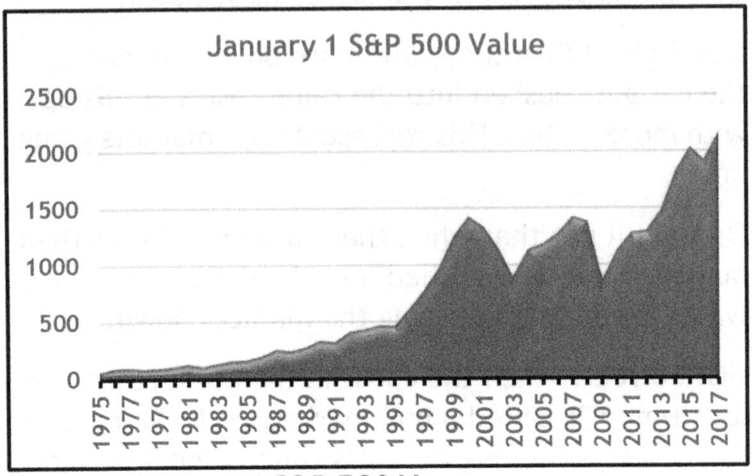

FIGURE 8 JANUARY 1 S&P 500 VALUE

Q: So how does this help you to invest?

GG: Knowing that the markets have always gone back above their previous peak keeps you from panicking during a bear market. It gets pretty scary when your assets are worth much less than they were previously.

Q: But you really need to be patient huh? It took six years to recover from the dot-com bubble bust.

GG: You bet. That's why I never tried to earn the money that I needed to live on by investing. Instead, I put my money into IRA accounts knowing it's there for the long term and can recover from prolonged bear markets.

Q: That brings me back to the question I asked earlier: How did you decide what to invest your money in?

GG: Each type of financial instrument has different strengths and weaknesses and I chose them based on their properties.

Stocks

GG: Stocks are my favorites.

Q: Why?

GG: Because successful companies grow and increase in value. If they also pay dividends and increase them over time, as most dividend-paying companies try to do, that adds to their appeal.

Q: How about the companies that don't do so well?

GG: They get acquired by the successful ones, or worse yet, they go out of business.

Q: Have you ever owned companies that went out of business?

GG: Sure, lots of them. But the successful ones grew enough in value to overcome the loss of capital from the unsuccessful ones that failed.

Q: How did you limit your losses?

GG: I never invested more than 2 percent of my assets in a single company.

That strategy also helped me to diversify my portfolio because I spread my investments over different types of companies.

Q: Why did you do that?

GG: Because when one sector of the economy wasn't doing well I hoped that a different one would do better.

Q: But stock prices are very volatile, aren't they?

GG: Absolutely, look at this chart.

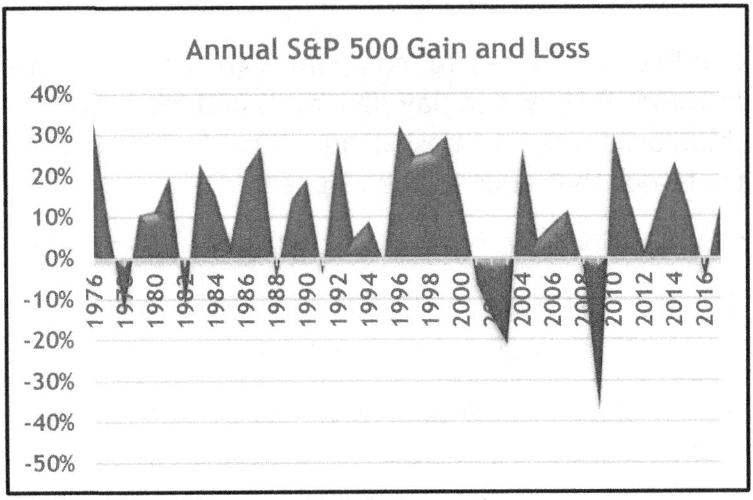

FIGURE 9 ANNUAL S&P 500 GAIN AND LOSS

Q: Whoa! That's a wild ride! How did you deal with it?

GG: When the markets were up, I was very happy. When they were down, I consoled myself by knowing that the Market RR Car would always fill up again.

To put it in a nutshell, the average annual gain of the S&P 500 over forty years was 9.1 percent. If you adjust for inflation it drops to 5.6 percent. I use 5 percent for my long-range financial planning and that number has stood up well over time.

And don't forget that the dividends compound if you reinvest them. Look at this chart.

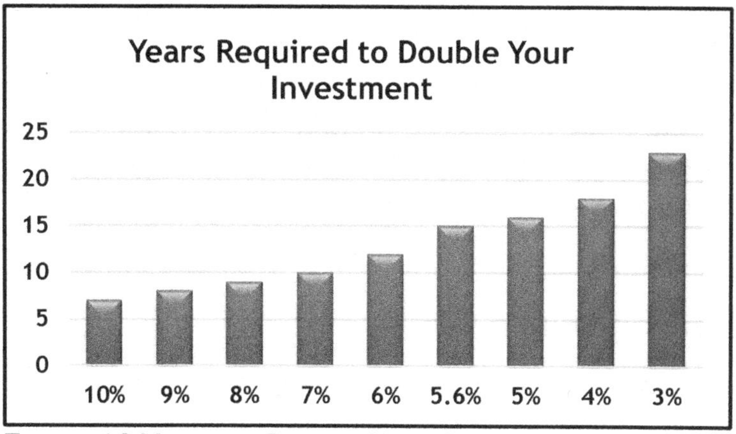

FIGURE 10 YEARS TO DOUBLE YOUR INVESTMENT

Q: From what I see, investments will double in eight years when the average annual gain is 9 percent and they will double in fifteen years using the 5.6 percent rate. Is that right?

GG: Yes, at 5.6 percent the actual purchasing power of your investments will double in 15 years. But look how long it takes at lower percentages. At 3 percent it takes twenty-three years.

That's why it's necessary to seek the highest return possible without taking on excessive risk and to minimize your investing expenses.

Bonds

Q: But aren't bonds less volatile than stocks?

GG: Normally they are—if they are high quality. But junk bonds can change value rapidly if the corporation or government that issued them runs into trouble.

Q: Why don't you like bonds as an investment?

GG: Because they don't take care of inflation well. When you hold them to maturity, the purchasing power of the returned principal is usually much less than it was when you purchased the bond.

And there is another reason too—they can get called.

Q: What does that mean?

GG: Well, suppose that you choose a high-quality bond that pays a really good interest rate. If the prevailing interest rate falls too far below the bond coupon rate, then the issuer redeems them and issues new bonds at the lower prevailing rate.

Q: So you end up not receiving the interest payments any longer. Instead you get your capital back and need to reinvest it at the lower prevailing interest rate.

GG: Right. It happened to me several times.

Q: But when the prevailing interest rate falls below the bond coupon rate, the bond increases in value. You can then sell it for a capital gain.

GG: You are right of course but you must actually sell it to lock-in the gain. That forces you into a buy low-sell high strategy and that was pretty unsuccessful for me, as I will talk about soon.

I like to invest in securities that I can hold for a long time and it's unusual to make an inflation-adjusted gain by holding a bond to maturity.

Q: What about investing in bond funds? You wouldn't have to buy and sell those.

GG: That's right, I could hold them as long as I wanted to and they are certainly less volatile than stocks.

But bond funds almost always gain less in value than stocks over the years. So instead of investing in bonds, I prefer to invest in dividend paying stocks.

Q: Why?

Dividend-Paying Stocks

GG: The dividends can go up over time whereas the bond interest payment is fixed for the life of the bond.

Dividends are usually measured as a percentage of the stock price. If the company is successful, its stock price will increase over time and the dividends rise along with it.

Meanwhile the capital that you initially invested in the stock stays constant, so if you calculate the dividend as a percentage of your initial investment it can increase significantly over the fixed rate that you would have received on a bond purchased with the same amount of capital.

Q: I see. You get to benefit from the potential capital gain as well as the dividends.

Money-Market Funds

Q: Do you invest in money-market funds?

GG: Yes. I find money-market funds to be a very convenient place to park money that I don't want to put at risk. They are available in both IRA and non-IRA accounts.

Q: But they don't pay much interest and there is no possibility for making capital gains because their price is maintained at one dollar—so why use them?

GG: Because they are highly liquid. It's very easy to move money into and out of them. And your capital is safe because they never drop below a dollar a share.

Q: Okay, now I understand the type of investments that you like. But what did you actually invest in?

Investing Strategies

My IRA Rollover

GG: When I left the corporate world in 1987, after working there for twenty-two years, my IRA was valued at $142,295.75. I rolled it into a trust at my local bank and invested it all in the "Trust Funds Treasury Portfolio - B"—a money-market fund.

By March 1988 I had made the following IRA investments:

200	Air Products and Chemicals
300	American Electric Power
100	Apple Computer
100	Bristol Myers Squibb
400	Equifax
200	H J Heinz
200	Johnson & Johnson
200	Microsoft
400	Public Service Enterprise Group
400	Waste Management
300	Weyerhaeuser
$ 14,015	Trust Funds Treasury Portfolio - B
$ 25,000	AXIA Fed C/D 7.15% Due 3/23/89
$ 25,000	AXIA Fed C/D 7.40% Due 3/23/90

FIGURE 11 MARCH 1988 IRA INVESTMENTS

Q: What happened next?

GG: Over the next few years I churned through lots of different investments trying to develop a strategy that I was comfortable with.

Q: What strategies did you try?

Buy Low, Sell High

GG: I first tried to follow the time-worn market adage of buy low and sell high but it didn't work for me. The major problem was that I really couldn't determine how low was low. Or when was high high enough.

If I bought a stock when I thought it was at its bottom and then it went lower I felt stupid. If I sold it for a gain then I worried about selling it too soon and missing out on further gains.

Q: So what did you do next?

Buy-and-Hold

GG: I bought stocks and didn't sell them. This is called buy-and-hold, and it solved the problem of selling them too soon. But it created another problem.

Q: What was that?

GG: I took some pretty heavy losses on companies that performed poorly.

I held them until their value was so low that I couldn't gain enough capital back from selling them to make the transaction worthwhile. So I just held on to them hoping they would recover. Often they didn't, and their stock became worthless.

Eventually I learned not to invest in companies that used unusual accounting techniques. However, this required me to carefully read the footnotes in their annual reports and that was a tedious and time-consuming process.

I also learned to quickly sell companies that became involved in scandals, legal imbroglios, or fraudulent activities. Their management gets so heavily involved in solving the problems they have created that they fail to stay focused on maintaining profitability.

Research

Q: How much time did you spend evaluating investments?

GG: Quite a lot—and it wasn't easy in the days before the Internet. I subscribed to the *Wall Street Journal* and the *Investor's Business Daily*—both of which ensured that I was always subjected to a barrage of typically bad news about the daily goings-on in the commercial world.

I also subscribed to *Value Line*. I received a weekly publication that focused on a set of stocks in a particular business segment. One week it might be manufacturing companies, the next week financial companies, and so on. After a thirteen-week period they cycled back to the initial business segment.

They evaluated companies and identified those that they considered over- or undervalued. I actually had a big binder and would dutifully replace the thirteen-week-old publication with the latest one after I read through it.

It all seems pretty quaint now.

Stockbrokers

Q: How about getting advice from your stockbroker?

GG: Stockbrokers only make money when they buy and sell stocks for you. They have no stake in your investment gains or losses so they really don't care if you make or lose money.

Disreputable ones, and there were legions of them, would "churn" your account with needless buying and selling. Their fees could really add up.

For example, the brokerage fee to buy or sell 100 shares of a stock was typically $35 in 1988. Adjusted for inflation, that would be over $70 in 2016. Compare that with today's typical online one-hundred-share transaction fee of seven dollars.

Mutual Funds

Q: Why didn't you invest in mutual funds and skip all your efforts to select individual stocks?

GG: Because they usually had very high management fees that were based upon a percentage of the aggregate value of all the assets in the fund. These fees could substantially reduce any fund asset gains. Furthermore, they always charged the same fees—even when the fund's performance was subpar.

In addition, a large number of funds charged a sales fee called a frontend load that could be as high as 8 percent of the amount that you invested in the fund.

I eventually did buy some funds that had low management fees but never any with a frontend load.

Q: So you really tried to minimize your investing expenses.

Investing Experiences

GG: Yes, I always tried to keep my costs of investing as low as possible because they could significantly reduce my gains.

Moving to Vanguard

GG: In 1993, I moved my IRA account to Vanguard.

Q: Why?

GG: Because Vanguard had the lowest fees of any company that I was aware of. It was owned by the people who invested in its assets, so there were no outside stockholders who required dividend payments.

Its founder, John Bogle, was a stickler for keeping costs down. In addition, their brokers, who at that time worked at an associated company named Wheat First Securities, executed only the orders that I initiated. They didn't hassle me with "churn" telephone calls.

Finally, and very important to me, Vanguard insured my account with adequate protection to cover all of my assets held there. So in the unlikely event that they went bankrupt, I wouldn't lose any money.

Here's a list of my assets when I moved them to Vanguard.

Five-Year Results

400	Air Products and Chemicals
100	Bristol Myers Squibb
200	H J Heinz
200	Johnson & Johnson
100	Lilly Eli & Co
100	Philip Morris
100	Colgate-Palmolive
400	Waste Management
100	Bank America
100	Computer Associates Intl
100	International Flavors & Fragrances
100	Gillette
100	Gerber Products
100	Engelhard
$30,077	Cash

FIGURE 12 SEPTEMBER 1993 IRA INVESTMENTS

Q: What were those assets worth at the time?

GG: $146,752.50.

Q: So you started with $142,295.75, and after five years of working really hard to invest successfully, you made a grand total of only $4,456.75—that's pathetic!

What happened with Microsoft and Apple, two of the greatest growth stocks of the twentieth and twenty-first centuries?

GG: I sold them during my buy-low-sell-high era. I invested $6,005 in Microsoft on March 22, 1988 and sold it on July 3, 1991 for $19,440. That was a gain of $13,435 and I considered that to be a very good profit at the time.

Q: What about the Apple shares?

GG: I also bought them on March 22, 1988 for $4,475 and sold them on January 3, 1991 for $4,300. So not counting inflation, I lost $175 on that one.

Q: I can understand the Microsoft sale, but why did you sell Apple?

GG: Well, remember that I was in the computer field. I followed the Microsoft versus Apple competition daily, and I was very concerned about who would win, because the software that I was developing was based upon Microsoft's operating system.

By 1990 the market was saturated with PC clones, and Apple was the only company selling Macs. In late May, Microsoft rolled out Windows 3. It was a graphical system that could run on all the PC clones in the world, so I figured that Apple was in trouble.

It was—and its stock price fell. I dithered for a while but finally decided to sell the Apple stock because I was afraid that it would fall even further.

It never occurred to me that Microsoft and Apple could both succeed. The Microsoft PC was primarily a business computer, and the Apple Mac was a personal consumer's computer, so their major market focus was in completely different segments—and I totally missed it.

Looking back now, I can see clearly that I shouldn't have sold either stock, but don't forget what I told you earlier—I've always had trouble seeing into the future.

Q: I see that you increased your Air Products and Chemicals shares by two hundred. Why did you choose to do that?

Stock Splits

GG: I didn't. The stock split—so my initial two hundred shares became four hundred.

Q: Why did the stock split?

GG: In those days companies wanted their share prices to stay low so that working mom-and-pop investors like me could afford to buy them. When their shares got too expensive, they would double the number of them and that would cut the stock price in half.

Q: Do you still own Air Products and Chemicals?

GG: Yes, it's one of the survivors from my buy low-sell high years that made it into my buy-and-hold era and it turned out to be a great investment.

You probably know that almost everyone likes to talk about their good investments, but most folks seem to keep pretty silent about their bad ones.

My Best Stocks

Q: So how well did you do with Air Products?

GG: I bought the initial two hundred shares on March 22, 1988 for $9,546.

On my Vanguard statement for March 2016, I had eight hundred shares. The additional six hundred shares came from the stock splitting twice.

By 2016 the total value of my initial Air Products investment had grown to $115,240. On an inflation-adjusted basis, that initial investment had increased by 493 percent.

Q: Very impressive. Did you make any other investments that you want to brag about?

GG: Sure. My all-time best single-stock investment was in Colgate-Palmolive. I bought the initial one hundred shares on February 5, 1992, for $4,770.

On my Vanguard statement for June 2016, I held 1,440 shares. The additional shares resulted from stock splits and dividend reinvestments, and the total value had grown to $105,408. On an inflation-adjusted basis, the initial investment had increased by 1,284 percent.

Q: Well, that's very impressive. Have you any more bragging-rights stories?

GG: Yes, one more—Johnson & Johnson.

I bought two hundred shares on March 22, 1988, for $8,580. On my Vanguard statement for October 2016, I held 840 shares. The additional shares resulted from two stock splits and dividend reinvestments and their value was $97,432. On an inflation-adjusted basis, the initial investment had increased by 556 percent.

Q: Those split stocks certainly turned out to be great performers.

GG: Yes, but companies don't normally split their stock any more.

Q: Why not?

GG: Because most informed investors no longer buy individual stocks, so there's no need to incur the expense of splitting them.

Q: Really? What do these investors buy now?

Index Funds

GG: Index funds.

Q: What are index funds?

GG: Collections of assets proportioned to those tracked by a popular index, such as the Standard and Poor 500.

Q: Who invented them?

GG: John Bogle. In 1976, he launched the Vanguard 500 Fund because he believed that by buying and holding a broad section of the market, you could do much better than by trying to pick individual stocks.

Many years of comparing the performance of index funds to those of actively managed funds, which try to pick winning stocks, have confirmed that he was right.

GG: The index funds don't constantly buy and sell securities or charge large management fees so their expenses are typically much lower than those of the managed funds.

In 2016, according to *Morningstar*, the average passive stock fund had an asset-weighted annual fee of 0.11 percent, while the average annual fee for actively managed US stock funds was 0.78 percent.

Almost all of my investments over the last few years have been in index funds.

Q: How do you decide which ones to invest in?

GG: Well, I no longer have to worry about limiting my investment in any one of them to 2 percent of my assets, because the funds themselves are broadly diversified.

I also don't have to worry about when to sell a badly performing stock, because if a company fails, it will simply be dropped from the index.

Q: And you no longer need to expend the huge amount of effort that you did previously when you were working so diligently to identify good individual stocks.

GG: Exactly.

Cash/Market Ratio

The first thing that I had to determine was how much to invest in the index funds and how much to keep in cash.

Q: What ratio did you decide upon?

In 2016, I tried to keep 20 percent in cash and 80 percent invested in the stock market.

Q: So you're willing to forgo the potential gain on the cash for your peace of mind. But how did you decide to use 20 percent for your cash holdings?

GG: Once I started receiving my RMDs, I decided to keep the next four years of their projected amounts invested as cash to cover distributions that I might have to take in a prolonged bear market. That way I had a much higher probability that I wouldn't have to sell my investments at distressed prices.

If you remember from our earlier discussion, the RMD is determined by dividing the year-end IRA value by a life-expectancy number that comes from a table provided by the government.

The formula that I use to calculate the cash percentage is to divide the numeral one by the number in that table for each of the coming four years. The cash percentage is the sum of those four fractions. It currently works out to be 19.3 percent.

The percentage actually increases each year as I get older. But because the RMD values are projected numbers anyway, it isn't worth my effort to try to use the precise percentage. I used 20 percent because it's much easier for me to compare my year-to-year investment performance by keeping a constant percentage in cash.

Q: Do you recommend that everyone use 20 percent?

GG: Certainly not.

I think that's way too conservative a strategy. While you are in your earning years I believe that you should use 0 percent because you need to get the maximum return on your investments in order to stay ahead of inflation.

You get little or no interest on the money that you put in a money market fund so you effectively remove it from your pool of growth money. As a consequence, I believe that you should delay moving assets into cash as long as it makes sense in your situation.

As I approached retirement age, I got more cautious. I retired at sixty-five, so four years before that I started using a percentage that resulted in keeping four years of living expenses less my pension and projected social security earnings in a money-market fund. That worked out to be 15 percent.

Q: How has this strategy worked out for you?

GG: Pretty well. Here's a graph showing how my investments did last year. It shows 2016 month-end values compared to the 2015 year-end values.

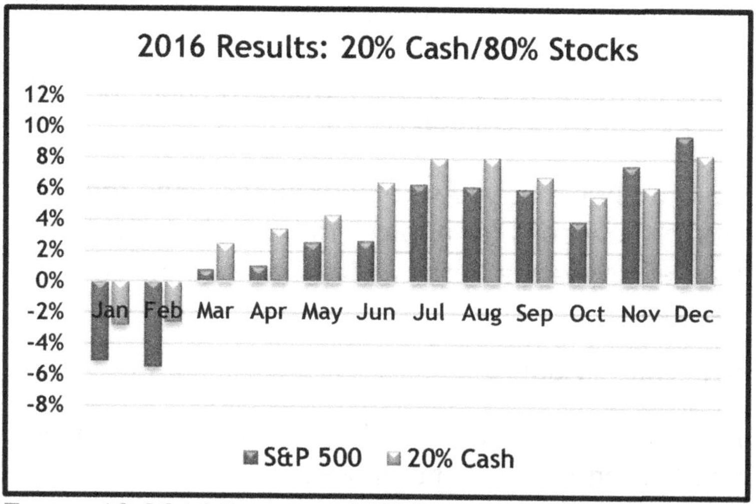

FIGURE 13 2016 RESULTS: 20% CASH/80% STOCKS

Q: It looks like your investments fell less when the market was down and they were worth more when the markets were up.

GG: Yes, except in November and December when I gave up some potential gains in the big market rally that occurred then.

But there's another benefit to maintaining a Cash/Market Ratio, even if you choose to use a less conservative percentage in cash.

Q: What's that?

GG: You know when to buy and sell.

Q: How?

GG: In a nasty bear market, when the Market RR Car is out in the desert for a long time, the value of the stocks fall, so my cash percentage exceeds 20 percent. I then buy indexed stock funds to restore the ratio back to 20 percent. That increases my gains as the markets recover when the bulls push the car back into the woods.

Q: And I bet that you sell index funds when the car sits in the woods for a long time and the roaring bull market drives the Cash/Market Ratio below 20 percent.

GG: That's right.

I'm back to a buy-low-sell-high strategy, but I now know when to make the moves.

Unique Opportunities

Q: I know that you invest mostly in index funds these days, but do you ever still buy individual stocks?

GG: Yes, sometimes the markets get so crazy that it's hard to pass up taking advantage of the situation.

I can give you two examples of buying individual stocks that turned out to be successful for me.

Q: What was the first one?

GG: In July 2008, during the deep bear market of the Great Recession, my total IRA value had fallen by 30 percent. I had confidence in my Market RR Car analogy, so I was certain that the markets would eventually recover.

Many financial institutions were failing because of a liquidity crunch that resulted from the bad housing-loan policies that I talked about earlier.

Bank stocks were deeply depressed and were selling at bargain-basement prices. The US Treasury and Federal Reserve were working around-the-clock to rescue the ones that had unwisely invested heavily in bad mortgages.

I was sure that the government wasn't going to let the too-big-to-fail institutions go bankrupt. So I bought shares in the largest bank in the country that was considered to be well managed and didn't hold massive quantities of toxic mortgages.

Q: What bank was it?

GG: JPMorgan Chase. At that time, the bank had a five-star S&P rating, and the quarterly dividends were yielding 4 percent.

I bought five hundred shares on July 1, 2008 for $36.13 each for a total investment of $18,066. Eight years later, in December 2016, those shares reached $85.79 and their value totaled $42,895—for a paper gain of $24,829 or 173 percent. That doesn't count the 2016 dividends, which were $920—5.1 percent of my initial investment.

Q: What was the second individual stock that you purchased?

GG: It was much more recent.

In December 2015, the price of oil crashed below $30.00 per barrel.

The financial press was all abuzz with dire oil overproduction forecasts indicating that the world was awash in the stuff. I knew that everyone in the world hadn't stopped driving their cars on the day before oil plunged that low, so it didn't make any sense to me.

I figured that the major producers would eventually have to curtail their overproduction in order to survive and that would result in raising the price of oil. As the price of oil recovered, the prices of the oil company stocks would rise as well.

I suppressed my bias against foreign stocks and on December 14, 2015 bought five hundred shares of Royal Dutch Shell for a total investment of $21,895. At that time, the annual dividends were over 7 percent.

A year later, in December 2016, the stock was $4,690 higher than I paid for it, and I had received $1,598 in dividends. That's a paper gain of 28 percent in one year.

Q: But these were pretty exceptional situations, right?

GG: Yes, the markets normally swing in a range of 0.5 percent a day and gradually drift higher or lower depending upon the direction that the Market RR Car is being pushed in. It's pretty unusual for things to get so crazy.

How to Invest

Q: Well, believing in your Market RR Car analogy, and using your Cash/Market Ratio to invest in index funds seems to be working well for you given all your years of experience.

But do you recommend it for other investors?

Using a Financial Adviser

GG: If they are ill at ease handling numbers, or they have limited access to the Internet, then they might need to have someone else manage their savings for them.

They should be wary of brokers masquerading as a financial adviser. These folks profit at their client's expense by recommending investments that generate the largest fees for themselves.

They should select a financial adviser who is a registered investment adviser. RIAs are required by law to act in their client's best interest. I highly recommend selecting an RIA who is also a certified financial planner.

Q: How can one find an RIA?

GG: They can search online for one at Investment Adviser Public Disclosure at http://bit.ly/FindAdv.

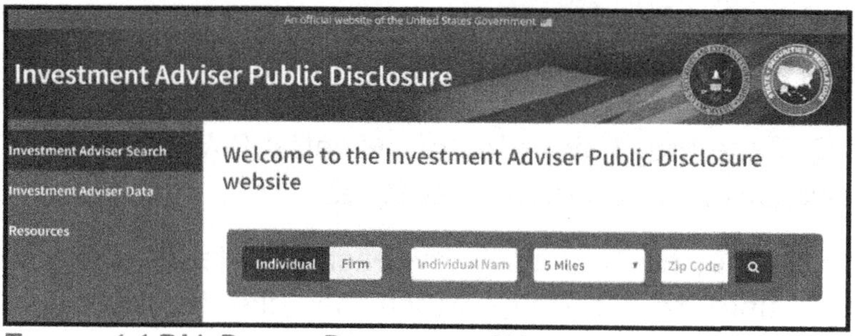

FIGURE 14 RIA PUBLIC DISCLOSURE WEBSITE

Every RIA is required to file Form ADV with the Securities and Exchange Commission. This website retrieves information from that form for those registered individuals or firms that are located within five, fifteen, or twenty-five miles of the zip code entered.

Q: How do investors decide which RIA to use?

GG: Since this is likely to be a lifelong relationship, selecting an RIA that they feel comfortable with is essential.

First, they have to determine if they just want advice to help them do their own investing, or if they want their RIA to actively manage their assets for them.

Next, they have to decide if they want to use an individual or a firm. The advantage of using an individual is that they may be more interested in achieving good results than an employee of a large firm might be.

If they choose a large firm, it's more likely to stay in business throughout their lifetime than if they use an individual. However, the person within the firm who is assigned to their account may change as the years go on.

Q: Once they have a list of potential RIAs from the website, what's their next step?

GG: They have to interview each one, face-to-face if possible, to determine which they like the best.

Q: What should they ask each potential RIA?

GG: Here's a list of questions:

1. Are you required by law to place my interests ahead of your own at all times? Are you willing to acknowledge your fiduciary duty in writing?
2. Where did you go to school? What training do you have in the investment management field?
3. What licenses do you hold?
4. Are you a certified financial planner? If the RIA claims to be a CFP® then visit the Certified Financial Planner Board of Standards website at http://www.cfp.net/ to confirm that they really are. Also check to see if their certification has ever been suspended or revoked.
5. How are you paid? Do you make more money if I buy a particular stock, bond, or mutual fund over another investment? If so, would you still recommend that investment and why?
6. What happens when you place an order for my account? Could I get a better price, or lower

cost, or commission if you sent my orders to a different market or broker to be executed?

7. Describe your typical client.
8. May I contact your long-term clients as references?
9. What is your investment philosophy? How does it differ from that of other investment advisers?
10. How often will we meet? How often will I receive written reports about my portfolio?
11. What other firms have you been registered with, and what is the status of those firms today?
12. Have you ever been disciplined by any government regulator for unethical or improper conduct or been sued by a client who was not happy with the work you did?

Q: Whew! That's a long list.

GG: I know. But it's really important to do a thorough selection job. Don't forget that the investor is going to entrust his or her entire lifetime's retirement savings with the RIA they choose.

Q: What about those folks who want to do their own investing?

Investing by Yourself

GG: If investors have good Internet access, and comparing numbers isn't a problem for them, it really is very straightforward today for people to manage their own investments.

Would you like to see how it's done?

Q: I'm not interested in dragging through a bunch of boring screen shots. How long is it going to take?

GG: Just a few minutes; the idea is to show you the decision-making process so you can learn to invest by yourself if you decide to.

I'm going use Vanguard's online system because that's the one that I'm familiar with. All the screen shots were taken from their website. Here's a shortened link to it http://bit.ly/Vangd.

Q: Do other consumer-oriented financial services firms have similar systems?

GG: Yes. It's a highly competitive industry and they all strive to maintain their websites at a comparable level.

Q: All right. I'll focus on trying to understand your strategies and not the screen shot details. Go ahead—but don't overdo it!

GG: My daughter has always contributed the maximum amount that she could into her company 401(k) plan and she's fortunate to benefit from receiving matching company contributions.

In 2016, for the first time since she lost her house, she was able to contribute an additional $5,500 into an IRA and that reduced her 2015 taxes as we talked about previously. She asked me to help her invest it.

Q: What did the two of you decide to buy?

GG: I'm going to take you through the whole process that we went through so that you can see how easy it is to invest with today's online technology.

GG: First, her Cash/Market Ratio percentage determines how much she should invest in index funds.

Q: Well, 20 percent of $5,500 is $1,100 so that leaves $4,400 for her to invest, right?

GG: No. She's many years away from retirement, so 0 percent is the right value for her. She needs to invest all $5,500 in the best growth fund that we can find.

Vanguard Online

Here's what her Vanguard account looked like after she entered her user name and password and logged on.

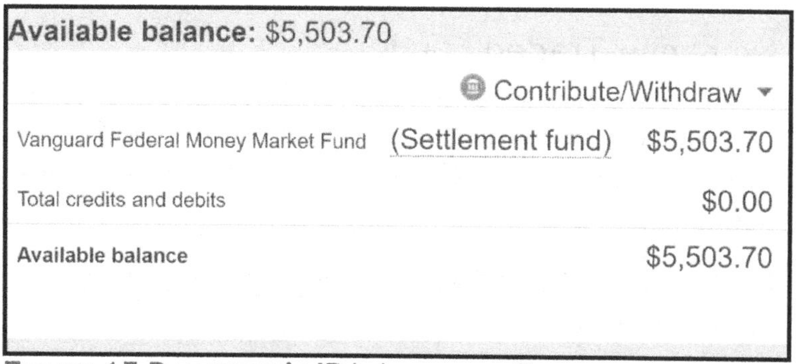

FIGURE 15 DAUGHTER'S IRA AVAILABLE BALANCE

She had already earned $3.70 in interest on her $5,500 deposit.

Q: What's a "Settlement fund?"

GG: That's where interest payments and dividends accumulate. It's also where the capital gains activities take place. When you buy funds, the money comes from this account, and when you sell funds, the money goes into it.

Q: What index funds were available to choose from to invest her $5,503.70 in?

When she clicked on the Investing tab at the top of her home screen here's what she saw.

Investment products	Account types
Vanguard mutual funds	IRAs: Roth & traditional
Vanguard ETFs	Individual & joint accounts
Other mutual funds	529 college savings plans
Stocks & other ETFs	Annuities
CDs & bonds	SEPs, SIMPLEs & i401(k)s

FIGURE 16 VANGUARD INVESTMENT PRODUCTS

Q: That's quite a lot to choose from. You talked about mutual funds previously, but what's an ETF?

Exchange-Traded Funds

GG: ETF stands for Exchange-Traded Funds. They are like mutual funds except that you can buy and sell them throughout the day whenever the markets are open.

Q: How does that differ from buying and selling mutual funds?

GG: You place an order to buy or sell a mutual fund during the day and it gets executed once the market closes and the value of the fund shares is calculated.

Q: What are the differences between the two?

GG: ETF share prices get recalculated throughout the day so you don't have to wait until the markets close to know what they are worth. You may also have to pay brokerage fees when you buy and sell them; however, Vanguard doesn't charge fees on its own ETFs.

It's nice to know the most current value of your investments whenever you log into your account so the ETFs have the advantage there. But since you are hopefully investing for the long term, the ETF's trigger-finger buying and selling advantage really shouldn't matter much.

Mutual funds are required to distribute their taxable capital gains at the end of each year and ETFs don't often distribute taxable capital gains. But since IRA account holdings aren't taxed until you withdraw from them, mutual funds and ETFs are essentially the same from a capital gains tax viewpoint.

Mutual funds, as well as some ETFs, allow you to automatically reinvest your capital gains distributions and dividends in additional shares. If you choose that option, you'll receive automatic compounding without having to worry what to reinvest in.

The biggest difference is that the minimum amount that you can invest in a Vanguard mutual fund is $1,000 whereas you can invest in an ETF for the cost of a single share.

Fund Analysis

Q: So how did you two evaluate potential investments?

GG: We started by having her click on the Vanguard mutual funds link.

Her next click was on the "Choose your mutual funds" tab and this screen popped up.

FIGURE 17 BUILD A PORTFOLIO

Since we were interested in saving for her retirement we clicked on the all-in-one fund link...

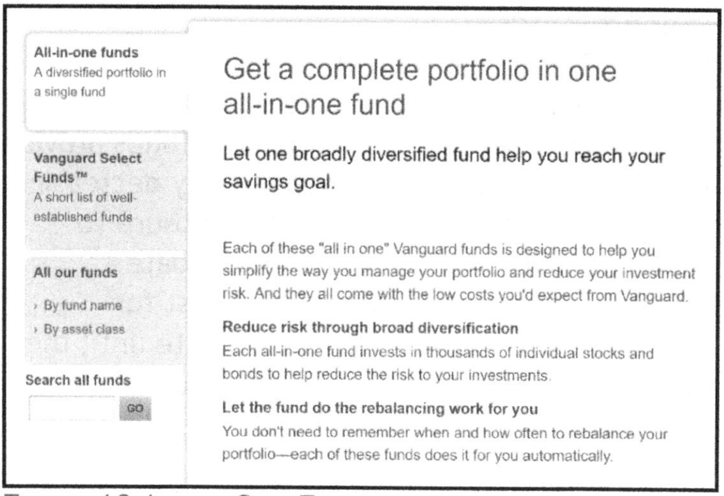

FIGURE 18 ALL-IN-ONE-FUND

Then, in the "Search all funds" field, she typed "Vanguard Retirement 2025."

Q: Why did she type that?

GG: Because that's what her 401(k) is invested in and we wanted to learn more about it. Here's what popped up.

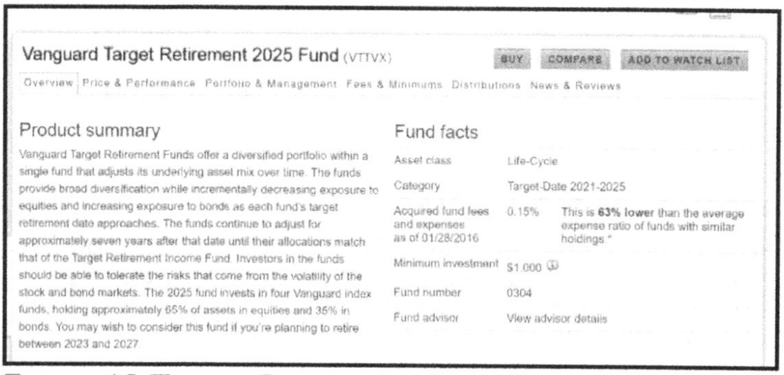

FIGURE 19 TARGET RETIREMENT 2025 FUND

It's pretty difficult to read the small screen-shot text. So here it is in a larger font:

Balanced Funds

"Vanguard Target Retirement Funds offer a diversified portfolio within a single fund that adjusts its underlying asset mix over time. The funds provide broad diversification while incrementally decreasing exposure to equities and increasing exposure to bonds as each fund's target retirement date approaches. The funds continue to adjust for approximately seven years after that date until their allocations match that of the Target Retirement Income Fund.

Investors in the funds should be able to tolerate the risks that come from the volatility of the stock and bond markets. The 2025 fund invests in four Vanguard index funds, holding approximately 65 percent of assets in equities and 35 percent in bonds. You may wish to consider this fund if you're planning to retire between 2023 and 2027."

Q: With all those bonds in it this fund-of-funds doesn't seem like it would be your cup of tea.

GG: Perhaps not. Vanguard's investment strategy for this fund is to dynamically split retirement assets between stocks and bonds.

Vanguard has accumulated vast experience in determining the risks acceptable to their account holders. This fund is obviously designed to fit the risk profile of many of their retirement investors.

However, if you are willing to take more risk, as I am, I believe that you can do better over long time periods by investing purely in stocks.

Vanguard has plenty of other funds to choose from so you can allocate your own investment money any way that you want to.

GG: My daughter paged down until she reached this.

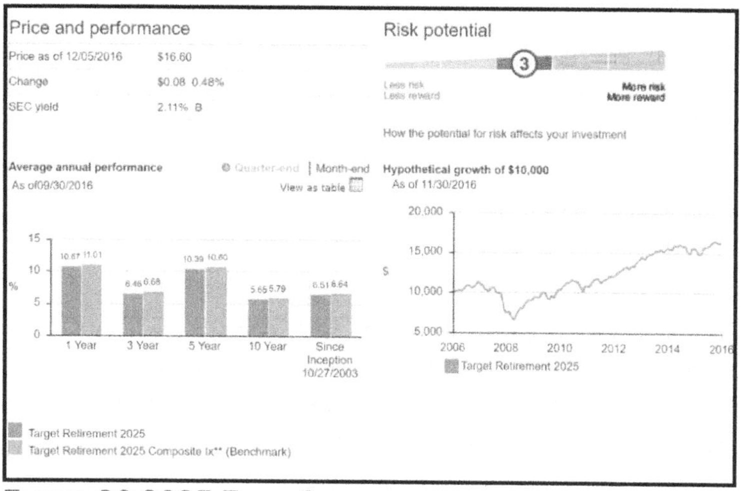

FIGURE 20 2025 FUND CHARTS

Q: What do all these charts mean?

GG: It's pretty hard to see them clearly in the screen shot, so I'll describe them one section at a time.

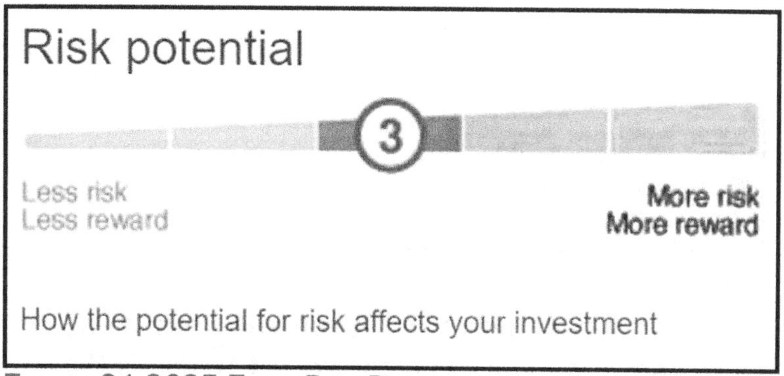

FIGURE 21 2025 FUND RISK POTENTIAL

The risk potential shows this fund to be about average, so swings of the fund's share price should be about the same as those of the overall markets.

Price and performance	
Price as of 12/05/2016	$16.60
Change	$0.08 0.48%
SEC yield	2.11% B

FIGURE 22 2025 FUND PRICE AND SEC YIELD

The SEC yield is the fund's projected annual dividends plus bond interest divided by its share price. The value of 2.11 percent is underwhelming. Even in the low-rate 2016 market, many other conservative funds did better.

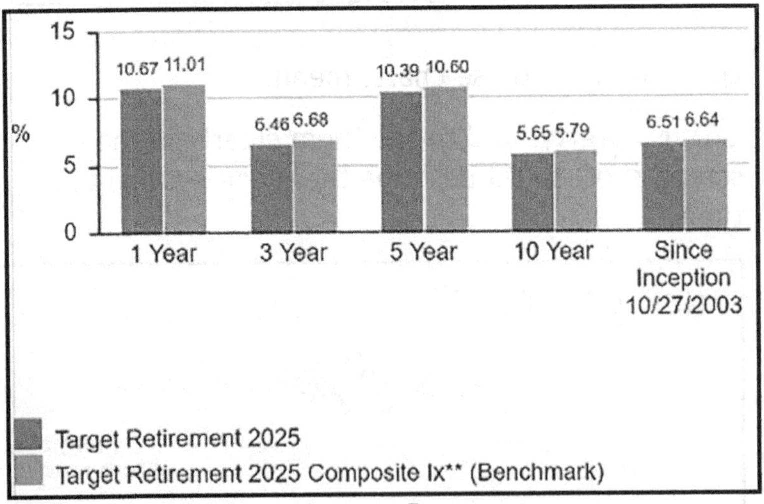

FIGURE 23 2025 FUND ANNUAL PERFORMANCE

For selecting a long-term retirement investment, I think that the most important chart to use is the

Average Annual Performance. Because funds begin their existence on different dates I prefer to use their ten-year performance to evaluate them rather than their gain since inception.

This fund's 5.65 percent ten-year annual return doesn't compare very favorably with the 9.1 percent S&P 500 average annual gain that we talked about earlier.

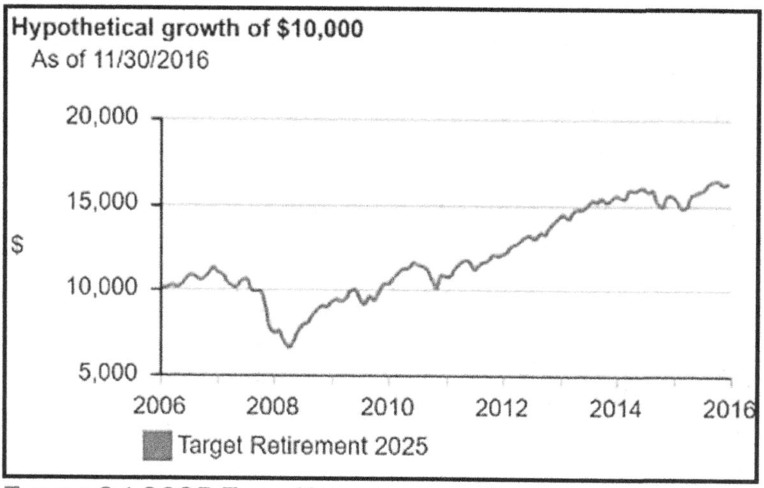

FIGURE 24 2025 FUND HYPOTHETICAL GROWTH

GG: This final feel-good chart shows how well you would do if you had invested $10,000 at the beginning of the selected time period. The chart numbers aren't adjusted for inflation so I don't usually pay much attention to them. In my opinion they lead you to believe that you will have more purchasing power in the future than you will really obtain by investing in the fund.

Q: So you wouldn't advise her to invest any more money in this fund?

GG: No.

GG: But this fund is the only one that she has to choose from in her 401(k) investment account. It's certainly not a bad investment by any means; however, I think that she can do better by selecting a different fund for her IRA account.

Notice how much useful information was available in these few charts. They allowed us to quickly determine if we wanted to invest any more of her precious savings in this fund. Compare that to the enormous effort that I had to expend in past years to find suitable investments.

Q: It certainly seems to be much easier now. What did you look at next?

GG: We went back to the "Vanguard mutual funds" page, chose the "Your funds" link and clicked on "Fund categories." There were 127 matching funds. She paged down until she got to the Stock funds section.

Stock Funds

				Price as of 12/05/2016				As of 12/05/2016	Average annual returns as of 11/30/2016			
Name	Ticker	Asset class	Expense ratio	Price	Change		SEC yield	YTD	1-yr.	5-yr.	10-yr.	Since inception
Stock funds												
Large-cap												
500 Index Admiral Shares	VFIAX	Stock - Large-Cap Blend	0.05%	$204.41	$1.20 ↑	0.59% ↑	2.11% B	10.07%	8.02%	14.41%	6.88%	5.12% (11/13/2000)
Diversified Equity	VDEQX	Stock - Large-Cap Blend	0.40%	$32.10	$0.28 ↑	0.88% ↑	1.20% B	7.54%	4.94%	13.81%	6.50%	7.33% (08/10/2005)
Dividend Appreciation Index Admiral Shares	VDADX	Stock - Large-Cap Blend	0.09%	$23.08	$0.10 ↑	0.44% ↑	2.20% B	11.00%	9.73%	—	—	6.96% (12/19/2013)
Dividend Growth CLOSED	VDIGX	Stock - Large-Cap Blend	0.33%	$23.65	$0.11 ↑	0.47% ↑	2.01% B	6.68%	5.04%	12.49%	7.93%	8.10% (05/15/1992)
Equity Income	VEIPX	Stock - Large-Cap Value	0.26%	$32.47	$0.17 ↑	0.53% ↑	2.75% B	12.17%	10.26%	13.76%	7.41%	10.09% (03/21/1988)
FTSE Social Index	VFTSX	Stock - Large-Cap Growth	0.25%	$14.17	$0.10 ↑	0.71% ↑	1.72% B	8.87%	6.54%	15.48%	8.01%	3.42% (05/31/2000)
Growth and Income	VQNPX	Stock - Large-Cap Blend	0.34%	$43.28	$0.29 ↑	0.67% ↑	1.84% B	10.53%	8.23%	14.97%	6.35%	9.92% (12/10/1986)

FIGURE 25 VANGUARD STOCK FUNDS

Since we were interested in finding the ones with the best ten-year returns, she double-clicked in that column's heading and this resorted screen appeared.

Name	Ticker	Asset class
Stock funds		
Large-cap		
S 500 Index Admiral Shares	VFIAX	Stock - Large-Cap Blend
Diversified Equity	VDEQX	Stock - Large-Cap Blend
Dividend Appreciation Index Admiral Shares	VDADX	Stock - Large-Cap Blend
Dividend Growth CLOSED	VDIGX	Stock - Large-Cap Blend

FIGURE 26 LARGE-CAP STOCK FUNDS

Q: Why are some of the funds closed?

GG: Vanguard closes their funds when they hold so much capital that Vanguard thinks they can't accept more and continue to maintain the fund's performance objectives. This policy protects the investors who already own them. As this screen shows, Vanguard has decided to close the Dividend Growth Fund.

We selected the best ten-year performing fund that was available to invest in—the Equity Income Fund. It has averaged a 7.63 percent return over ten years. In addition, its Year-to-Date return is 12.17 percent and that looks very good. So we decided to investigate in more depth by clicking on the link to it.

Here are the same informative charts that we looked at previously.

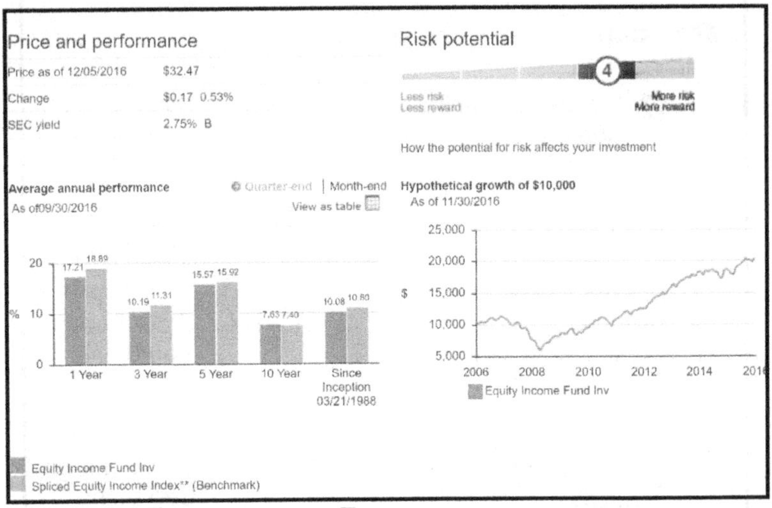

FIGURE 27 EQUITY INCOME FUND

Q: Well, its SEC yield of 2.75 percent is higher and it seems to be doing very well this year with an average annual performance of 17.21 percent. Did you choose to invest in this one?

GG: Not yet. I like to dig deeper into a fund before I decide to invest in it. Here's the description of this fund:

"This fund is designed to provide investors with an above-average level of current income while offering exposure to the stock market.

Since the fund typically invests in companies that are dedicated to consistently paying dividends, it may have a higher yield than other Vanguard stock mutual funds.

The fund's emphasis on slower-growing, higher-yielding companies can also mean that its total return may not be as strong in a significant bull market. This income-focused fund may be appropriate for investors who have a long-term investment goal and a tolerance for stock market volatility."

Q: That sounds like something you would be interested in investing in.

GG: It looks very promising but the risk level is only four and we decided to search for some risk level-five funds to compare this one with.

Small-Cap Funds

She searched using the ten-year performance until she found the Vanguard Tax-Managed Small-Cap Fund. Here's what the charts for that one look like.

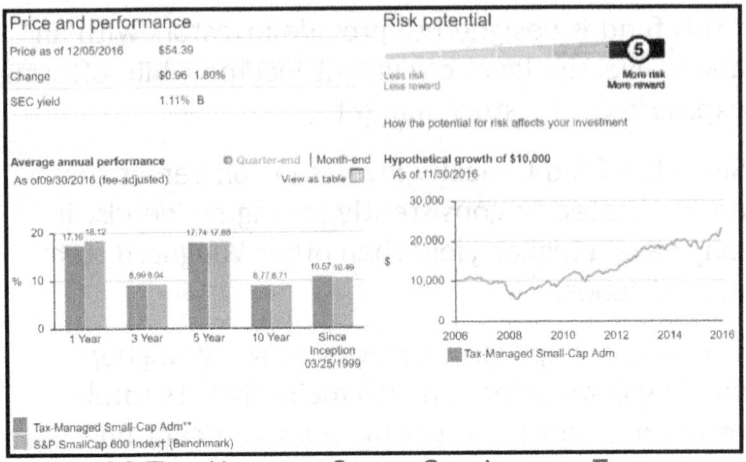

FIGURE 28 TAX-MANAGED SMALL-CAP ADMIRAL FUND

Q: The ten-year performance of 8.77 percent is much better.

GG: You are right. So we decided to find more details about it. Here's the description of the fund.

"As part of Vanguard's series of tax-managed investments, this fund offers investors exposure to small-capitalization stocks. Its unique, index-oriented approach attempts to track the benchmark, while keeping taxable gains to a minimum.

One of the fund's risks is its focus on small-cap companies, which can be a volatile segment of the market. Investors in higher tax brackets who have an investment time horizon of five years or longer and a high tolerance for risk may wish to consider this fund complementary to a well-balanced portfolio."

It seemed to be just the ticket for her. Unfortunately, the fund's minimum investment is $10,000 and that's out of her league.

Q: So what did you do next?

Evaluating ETFs

GG: Since she was priced out of the fund, we looked into ETFs. She found this one for small-cap stocks.

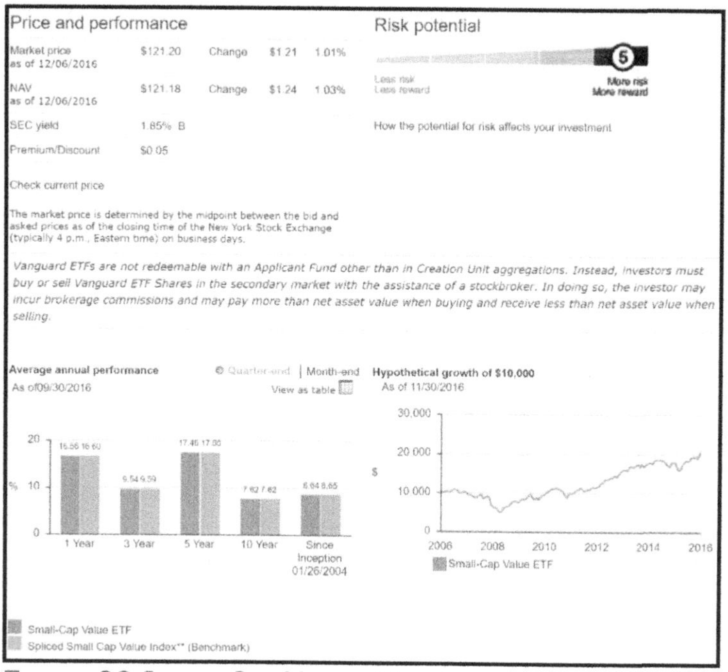

FIGURE 29 SMALL-CAP VALUE ETF

While not quite as good as the small-cap fund, this Risk-Potential-Five small-cap ETF looks good with its ten-year performance of 7.62 percent.

Q: What does small cap mean?

GG: A company's market capitalization is the total value of its outstanding shares. Vanguard assigns its small-cap designation to companies in the $3 billion range.

Clicking the Portfolio and Management tab produced this screen.

Portfolio

Stock style

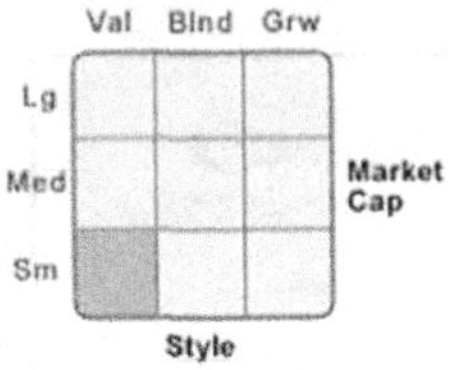

Vanguard Small-Cap Value ETF seeks to track the performance of a benchmark index that measures the investment return of small-capitalization value stocks.

Learn more about this portfolio's investment strategy and policy.

What is this?

Equity characteristics as of 10/31/2016

	Small-Cap Value ETF
Number of stocks	859
Median market cap	$3.1 billion
Price/earnings ratio	22.2x
Price/book ratio	1.8x
Return on equity	10.5%
Earnings growth rate	7.3%
Foreign holdings	0.3%
Turnover rate (as of fiscal year end December)	15.5%
Short-term reserves	—
Fund total net assets	$20.5 billion
Share class total net assets	$8.1 billion

FIGURE 30 SMALL-CAP VALUE ETF PORTFOLIO

Q: What do all those figures mean?

GG: They are measures of the assets held in the ETF. When analyzing individual companies, they are worth digging into. But for a fund or ETF they aren't very useful for making investment decisions because they are an aggregate of values from all the companies—in this case 859 of them.

However, there is one measure that's important to me. I usually don't like to invest in foreign holdings because my years spent in international business taught me that companies outside the United States are more likely to "cook their books" in order to make their performance appear better than it really was.

Fortunately, with only 0.3 percent of these companies outside America, this fund looks good from that perspective.

Scrolling to the next screen provides some really useful information.

Equity sector diversification

	Small-Cap Value ETF as of 10/31/2016
Basic Materials	5.30%
Consumer Goods	6.60%
Consumer Services	10.40%
Financials	30.90%
Health Care	5.60%
Industrials	20.80%
Oil & Gas	5.10%
Other	0.00%
Technology	8.40%
Telecommunications	0.40%
Utilities	6.50%

FIGURE 31 ETF SECTOR DIVERSIFICATION

Q: What does this tell you?

GG: It shows how the stocks held in the ETF are spread among different industries. This fund is very well diversified except for Telecommunications and I suspect that's due to the fact that most telecommunication companies are very large, hence don't fit into the small-cap category. But it certainly looks like a great ETF for my daughter to invest in.

Q: So did she decide to buy it?

GG: Well, it was a difficult decision for her. The fund's ten-year performance was 8.77 percent versus the ETF's 7.62 percent, so the fund performed 1.15 percent better. As we spoke about earlier, that much percentage difference can make a significant impact over many years.

Of course, you have to assume that the fund's performance advantage will be maintained in the coming years. There's no way to know if it will or will not because its past history may not be repeated. However, she has to choose something to invest in, and the historical record is all that she has to go on.

Q: But the fund requires a minimum investment of $10,000 and your daughter only has $5,500 to invest. What did she do?

GG: She decided to invest initially in the ETF. Her money was stagnant while sitting in the money-market fund and she wanted it to start growing.

If she is able to add $5,500 to her IRA in 2017, and the ETF grows in value, she will have more than needed for a fund requiring the $10,000 minimum investment. She can then sell the ETF and buy the best ten-year performing mutual funds or ETFs that she can find at that time.

Because the ETF is in an IRA account there won't be any capital gains tax to pay when she sells it, so her capital will be preserved.

If she is unable to contribute enough to her IRA in 2017 to reach $10,000, she will add more money to the ETF in future years until its value reaches that amount. In the interim, the money that she has invested in the ETF will continue to grow.

Q: That seems like a very practical strategy.

GG: Well, she's a smart kid, and she has learned a lot since her house disaster.

Buying and Selling

Would you like to see how she made her investment in the ETF?

Q: Since you've already dragged me through all these screens, I guess I'll have to learn how she did it.

GG: First, she clicked on her "My Accounts" tab, then the "Balances & holdings" link, and finally the "Buy and sell" link in the upper left corner.

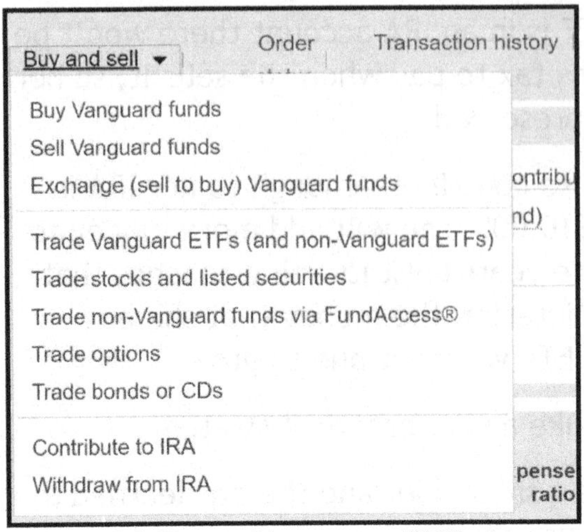

FIGURE 32 TRADE VANGUARD ETFS LINK

She clicked on the "Trade Vanguard ETFs" link and clicked on "Transaction type."

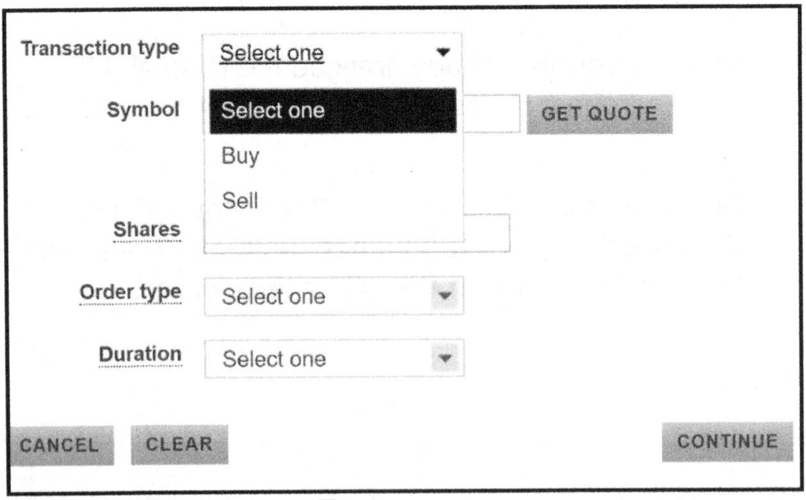

FIGURE 33 TRANSACTION TYPE

She wanted to buy this ETF so she chose "Buy." She couldn't remember the ETF's symbol so she clicked on the "Look up symbol" link and that displayed as follows.

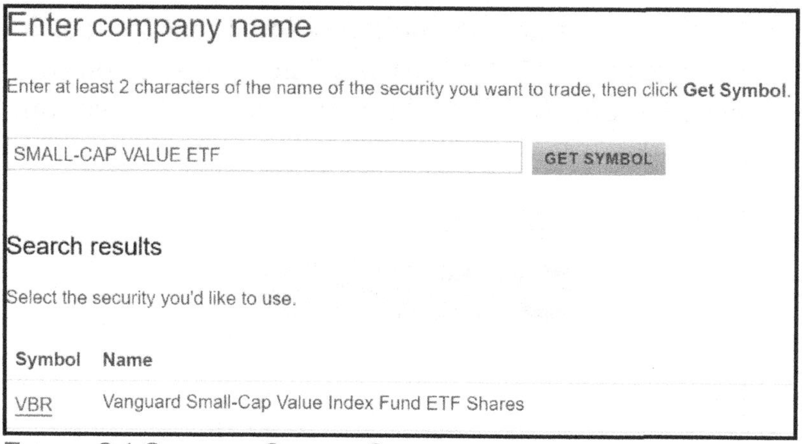

FIGURE 34 COMPANY SYMBOL SEARCH

She typed in "Small-cap value ETF" and clicked "Get symbol." Then she clicked on VBR, entered $5,500 in the Dollars to shares calculator, and clicked "Calculate."

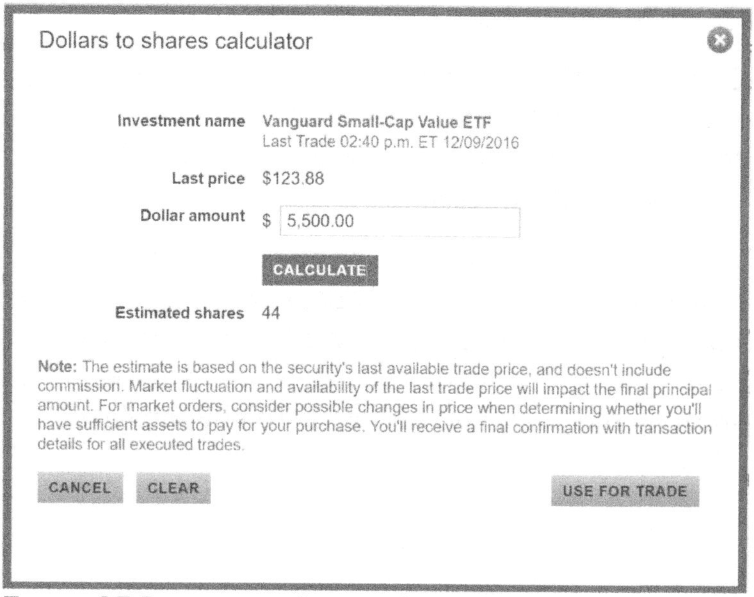

FIGURE 35 DOLLARS TO SHARES CALCULATOR

This showed that she could buy forty-four shares. So she clicked the "Use for trade" button; then on the next screen, she clicked the "Order type" selection.

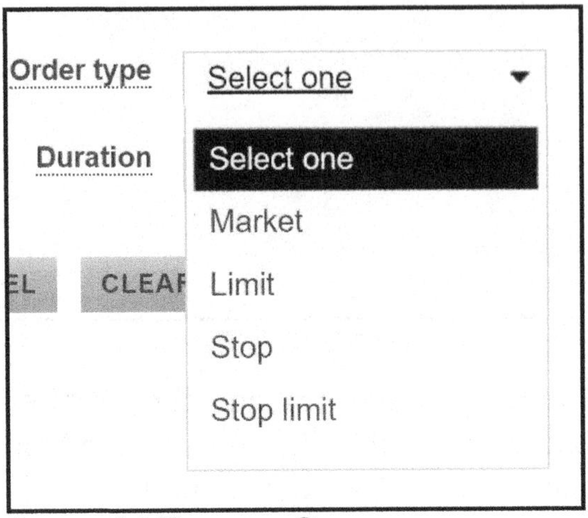

FIGURE 36 TYPES OF ORDERS

Q: What are all those types of orders?

GG: "Market" is for immediate execution. The others are more complicated ones used by market traders to control when their orders execute. I'll tell you more about them later.

Because my daughter is going to hold her ETF for a long time she doesn't care about precisely timing how the order is executed. So she selected "Market" to buy the ETF immediately. Here is the screen showing the details of her order to buy the ETF.

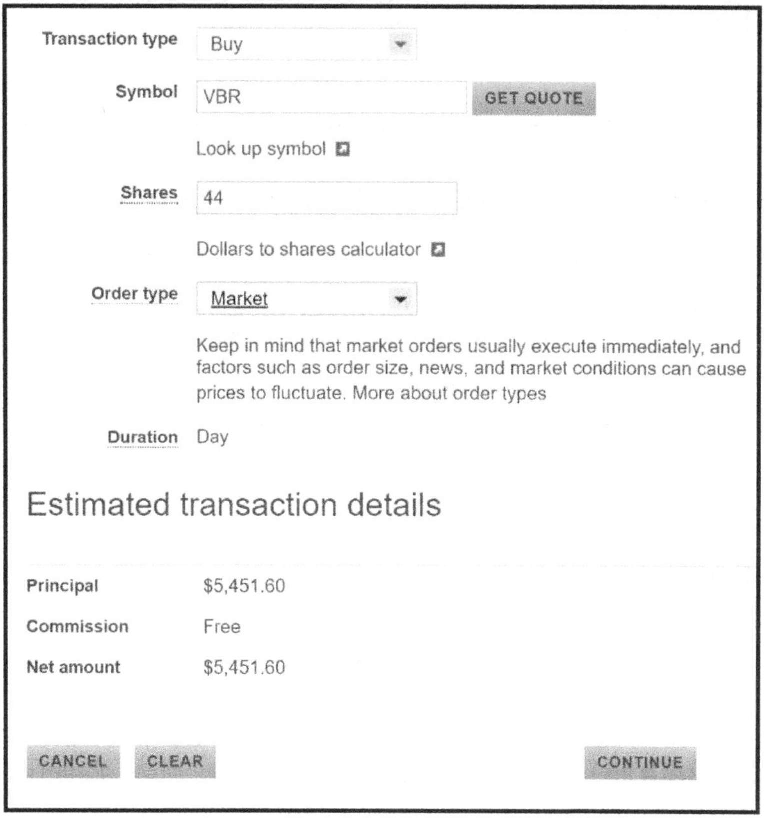

FIGURE 37 ESTIMATED TRANSACTION DETAILS

Because it's a Vanguard ETF there is no commission required to buy it.

The information looked fine to her so she clicked "Continue" and then "Submit" on the subsequent screen.

She wanted to know exactly what happened with her order, so she clicked the "Go to order status" link and this screen appeared.

Refresh | Get a quote | GO

Order date	Status	Symbol	Name	Transaction type	Dollars/Shares	Executed price	Action
12/09/2016	Executed	VBR	VANGUARD SMALL CAP VALUE ETF	Buy	44.000	$123.8896	—

FIGURE 38 ORDER STATUS

So she bought the VBR ETF for $123.8896 a share.

Her final objective was to make sure that the dividends from the ETF were reinvested automatically so she clicked on her "Trading profile" link and this screen displayed.

Services

Agreement for	Status
Options trading	No/No papers
Margin trading	No
Account dividend and capital gains election	Reinvest

FIGURE 39 TRADING PROFILE SETTINGS

As you can see, the dividends and capital gains are set to reinvest automatically so the ETF that she just purchased will reinvest automatically.

Q: Was she finished now?

GG: Yes, and she won't have to do anything else until she adds more money into her IRA next year.

Annuities

Q: You haven't talked about annuities yet. What are they?

GG: From an insurance industry perspective, they are like reverse whole-life insurance policies.

Whole-life policies use the money collected from those who live longer to pay the policy owners of those who die younger.

Annuities use the money collected from those who die younger to pay those who live longer.

Q: How about from a retiree's perspective?

GG: They are complex financial products.

Basically, you invest money, have it increase each year without paying taxes, and then trigger a stream of future payments on a timetable you can control. Those payments are taxed as ordinary income.

Insurers make money on annuity fees and management services. As they invest your money, they get to keep anything above the payments that they have guaranteed you.

Unlike IRAs, there is no income limitation on how much money you can invest in an annuity. However, if you decide you no longer want it, the surrender charges for an annuity can be very expensive.

In addition, you will have to pay taxes on any amount withdrawn that exceeds the amount you have invested in it.

And just like social security, after they've settled any payment obligations to your heirs, the insurers keep the remaining funds in your annuity contract once you've passed away.

Since I don't charge myself any management fees, I believe that I can get better returns by doing my own investing.

Furthermore, my IRA will pass to my daughter at its full value—and that's very important to me, especially with all the health problems that I have experienced.

For those folks who have others manage their money, annuities can be useful for holding a portion of their retirement savings.

If they need the security of receiving regular monthly payments, a good rule to follow is to buy an annuity that provides enough for basic monthly living expenses after subtracting other income such as social security and pension payments.

But they should also diversify into other types of investments because inflation is going to reduce the purchasing value of their monthly annuity payment as they get older.

Reverse Mortgages

Q: What about reverse mortgages?

GG: Some financially strapped folks who are sixty-two and older living here in my retirement community have used them.

Simply put, they sold their home to a mortgage company so they can continue to live in it, without making any monthly mortgage payments, until they move out or die.

They used the money from the reverse mortgage to pay off their conventional mortgage. They also used any excess to help pay their living expenses, including their property taxes and homeowners' insurance, which they are still responsible for.

They are also responsible for maintaining their homes to a reasonable level. The mortgage companies are diligent about inspecting them periodically and these folks have found the inspections to be quite annoying.

The reverse mortgage is charged interest that is treated as a loan advance. Each month the interest is calculated not only on the amount they received, but also on the interest previously assessed to the loan.

The biggest problem with a reverse mortgage is that the interest compounds over its lifetime. That means the mortgage may eventually exceed the market value of the house.

However, with an FHA-insured reverse mortgage, the borrower can never owe more than the value of the property and cannot pass on any debt from the reverse mortgage to any heirs.

Q: So reverse mortgages really aren't an investment in the sense that they are something that you buy to appreciate or generate income.

GG: No. They are more like a last-ditch bailout for those unfortunate folks who didn't save adequately for their retirement.

Q: Well, I hope I won't ever have to get one.

Reviewing My Investments

Q: How often do you check the value of your IRA holdings?

GG: Monthly. Vanguard emails me when the month-end statement is ready. To view it, I log on to my account, select the "My Accounts" tab and click on the "Statements" link. I click on the latest statement and get the PDF downloads for me to look at.

Q: How many years does Vanguard keep your online statements for?

GG: Ten years. So you don't have to worry about saving them unless you want to keep a really long history of your account.

Q: Do you go online to peek at your account between monthly statements?

GG: If I have extra time on my hands I sometimes look at it when the markets have a stellar up-day. It's my feel-good-for-a-day activity.

But I never do it when the markets are down because it depresses me. I know that the bulls will eventually push the Market RR Car back into the woods and that I'll be fine.

Rebalancing My Portfolio

Q: You must feel pretty good about your IRA investing results in 2016. You managed to outperform the S&P 500 for ten out of twelve months and made 8.3 percent on your investments.

GG: I did okay, but I could have done much better. Look at this chart.

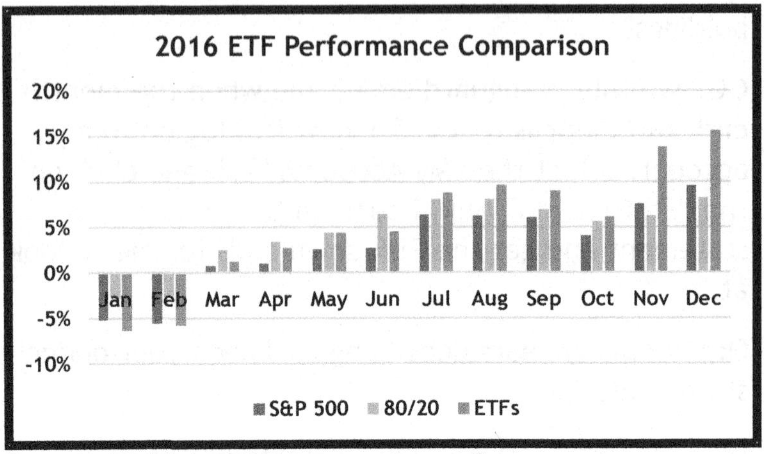

FIGURE 40 2016 ETF PERFORMANCE COMPARISON

Switching to ETFs

It compares my results with the performance of the top seven Vanguard Stock ETFs. They finished the year with a 15.6 percent gain—nearly double mine.

Q: Wow! How did you make the performance comparison?

GG: I made a simulated investment on January 1 by holding four years of my projected RMDs in cash and invested the balance in the seven top-performing stock ETFs. Then I tracked the performance of the seven ETFs monthly through the balance of 2016.

Q: Which ETFs did you use?

GG: Here's a table of them.

Ticker	Name	Yield	Gain
VTV	Value ETF	2.5%	13.9%
VYM	High Dividend Yield ETF	3.1%	13.3%
MGV	Mega Cap Value ETF	2.6%	13.5%
	Total Large Cap	2.7%	13.6%
VXF	Extended Market ETF	1.3%	14.4%
VOE	Mid-Cap Value ETF	2.1%	12.9%
	Total Mid Cap	1.7%	13.7%
VBR	Small-Cap Value ETF	1.9%	22.4%
VB	Small-Cap ETF	1.5%	16.4%
	Total Small Cap	1.7%	19.4%
	Total	2.1%	15.6%

FIGURE 41 2016 BEST-PERFORMING STOCK ETFS

Q: How did you decide how much to allocate to each ETF?

GG: It was very simple. Since there were seven ETFs I just divided the total money that I decided to invest in stocks by seven and invested that amount in each one.

Q: Why didn't you do this years ago?

GG: I was hanging on to my old favorite stocks. They were doing well and I felt comfortable with them.

Q: How many did you own?

GG: Forty-six.

Q: So what did you do next?

GG: I decided to sell all my individual stocks and invest in ETFs instead.

Q: How did you decide when to sell them?

Water Strider Metaphor

GG: Good question. I used my water strider metaphor.

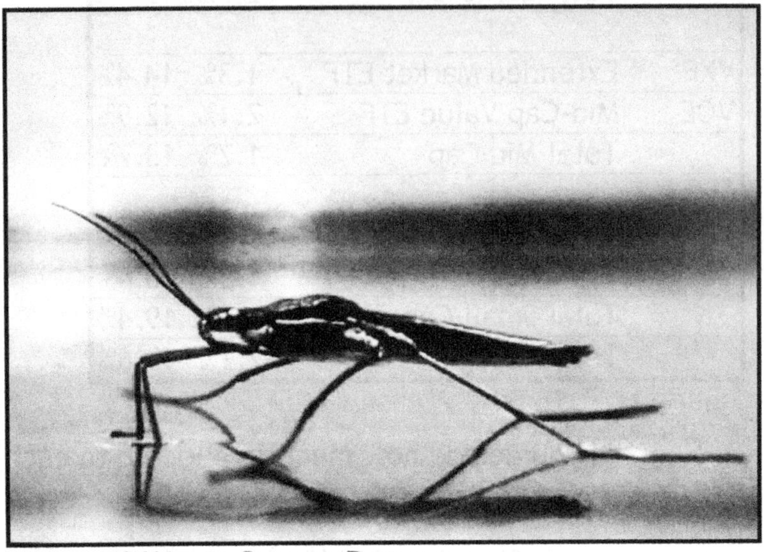

FIGURE 42 WATER STRIDER PICTURE

Individual stocks are like these bugs. They dance on top of the water in the Market RR Car. As the car fills up their prices rise, and as the water evaporates their prices fall.

The ripples on the water's surface represent the daily market movements. The smaller, younger bugs move rapidly with them while the larger, older bugs move more slowly.

A failing company is a dying bug that sinks. A hostile takeover is a water strider that's being eaten by a praying mantis. A large bird picking off one of the bug's legs is government overregulation.

I could go on but I'm sure that you get the idea.

Q: Cute, but how does that help you decide when to sell your stocks.

GG: I know for sure that the stock prices are going to go up and down as the Market RR Car moves. But because I'm a total failure at predicting when those market moves will happen, I'm going to let the market's historical price movements for each stock help me by using a limit order. I'll set it at the highest value that the stock hit in the previous fifty-two weeks.

Using Limit Orders

Q: What's a limit order?

GG: An order to sell a stock at a fixed price.

Would you like to see how one is placed?

Q: This sounds interesting.

GG: Here is screen shot similar to the one we saw when my daughter bought her ETF, but now I'm selling 280 shares of Walmart using a sell limit order.

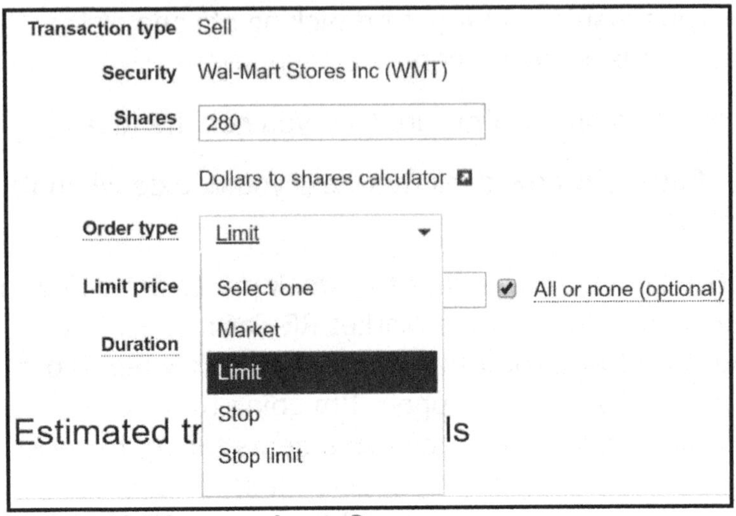

FIGURE 43 WALMART LIMIT ORDER

I selected the Good till Canceled (GTC) order duration so it would remain in effect for sixty days.

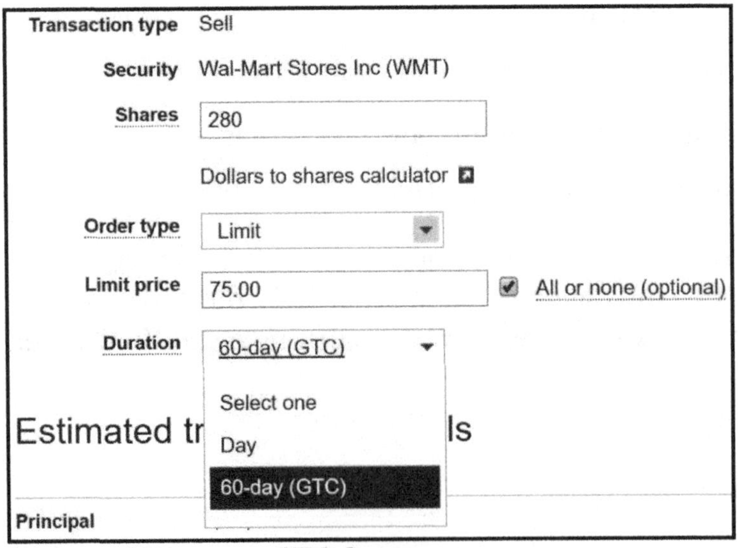

FIGURE 44 WALMART GTC ORDER

This order will trigger when (and if) Walmart hits $75.00 per share. Its highest price within the last fifty-two weeks was $75.19, which happened on August 18, 2016.

I also clicked the "All or None" box because I'm selling more than one hundred shares and I want to sell them all.

Q: But couldn't a stock go higher than its fifty-two-week peak value?

GG: Yes, it certainly could, but as you know by now my view of the future is always opaque—I have no ability to predict stock price movements.

Argus Stock Analysis

GG: Fortunately for me there are folks who spend their lives forecasting stock prices. When I was able to find a future price forecast from a reputable source that exceeded the stock's peak fifty-two-week value then I used that forecast price.

Q: What reputable source did you use?

GG: Vanguard provides detailed reports from Argus for most large companies. To find them, you click on the "Investing" tab, then click "Stocks & Other ETFs," and key in the ticker symbol. That takes you to a screen summarizing the stock and then you click the "Analyst reports" tab.

Here's the Argus opinion on JPM.

Analyst opinion details

Argus

12 Month rating	Buy
5 Year rating	Buy
Sector rating	Overweight
Financial strength	High
Target price	$97.00

FIGURE 45 ARGUS JPMORGAN CHASE OPINION

GG: Here's their investment thesis.

"JPM: Raising target price to $97 following 4Q EPS, on January 13, JPM reported 4Q16 EPS of $1.71, up from $1.32 in the prior-year quarter and $0.27 above consensus. Highlights for the quarter included strong core loan growth and healthy trading revenues. Our target price of $97 (raised from $78) assumes a multiple of 14.9-times our 2017 EPS estimate. We believe a recent revaluation of large bank stocks, on the potential for a less strict regulatory environment following a change in presidential administration, has merit."

GG: If you really want to dig into the details, you can download their detailed PDF file, but I just used their recommended price. If it turns out to be too high and the stock doesn't sell, I can always adjust the limit order to use a lower price.

Since JPM's highest price in the last fifty-two weeks was $88.17 on January 13, 2017, and the Argus price forecast is $97.00, I placed my JPM limit order at $97.00.

Q: What did you do with the stocks that had Argus "sell" forecasts on?

GG: I sold them using market orders that executed immediately.

Dollar-Cost Averaging

Q: Okay, now I understand your stock-selling strategy but what strategy are you going to use to buy the ETFs?

GG: I'm using dollar-cost averaging. I'm going to invest one-twelfth of my total for stocks in ETFs each month. That way I will forgo some gains if the market is really strong throughout 2017, but I will obtain lower average costs if the market fluctuates monthly or goes down.

Q: Well, it seems like you have a pretty good plan.

Autopilot Portfolio

GG: Yes, I hope so. But there's another benefit to moving into the ETFs.

Q: What's that?

GG: By the end of the year, all my individual stocks will be sold, and my ETF investments will be completed. Then my entire portfolio will be on autopilot.

My daughter isn't a numbers person, so she won't have to make any further investment decisions when she eventually inherits my IRA.

Q: I'm sure that she will appreciate that.

GG: But I'm going to miss my dear old stock friends because I've followed them for so many years.

However, I do have some solace knowing that I'm invested in thousands of stocks instead of just my forty-six water striders.

Closing Comments

Q: You know, with all the effort you've put into investing over the years, it seems to me that you should be worth more.

GG: Amassing a huge fortune didn't really appeal to me.

Like everyone else, I had to reduce my spending in the present in order to save money for my future retirement. But I wasn't interested in saving more than the maximum tax-sheltered amount.

I wanted to enjoy my life as much as possible while I was living it. Instead of expending the effort needed to accumulate great wealth, I preferred to spend my time enjoying my other pursuits.

I believe that amassing huge wealth in order to impress people is a silly game. With only one exception, there's always someone who's richer than you are.

Q: Who's the exception?

GG: The wealthiest person on the planet.

GG: My little pension, plus the social security payments that I receive, combined with my annual RMD provide more than enough for me to live on.

Q: What do you do with your extra money?

GG: I travel the world. I've been around it four times and have visited seventy-six countries.

Q: Where are you going next?

GG: I'm going to go play some tennis. It's a beautiful day here, and I'm looking forward to getting some exercise.

Q: But you're seventy-six. Isn't that a little old to be playing tennis?

GG: Nope. Relatively speaking, I'm just a youngster. Our oldest club member is eighty-seven, and he plays very well for his age.

You know what else? He's still working.

Q: Are you kidding me! He's still working at eighty-seven?

GG: Yeah, he never saved enough for his retirement years.

Glossary of Retirement Terms

Source: US Department of Labor, Bureau of Labor Statistics; Glossary of Employee Benefit Terms at http://bit.ly/EmpTerms.

Retirement Plans

Retirement plans are classified as either defined benefit or defined contribution plans.

Defined Benefit Plans

Defined benefit plans determine payments according to a fixed formula based on salary, years of service, and age.

Traditional defined benefit formulas

Percent of terminal earnings formulas. Benefits are based on a percentage of average earnings during a specified number of years at the end of a worker's career (or when earnings are highest), multiplied by the number of years of service recognized by the plan.

Percent of career earnings formulas. Benefits are based on a percentage of an average of career earnings for every year of service recognized by the plan.

Dollar amount formulas. Benefits are based on a dollar amount per month for each year of service recognized by the plan.

Percent of employer contribution formulas. Benefits are based on employer and, occasionally, employee contributions. Benefits equal a percentage of total contributions.

Benefit payment methods

Payments from defined benefit plans may be in the form of a straight life annuity, a joint-and-survivor annuity, a percentage of the unreduced accrued benefit, or a lump sum.

Straight-life annuity. A periodic payment made for the life of the retiree, with no additional payments to survivors.

Joint-and-survivor annuity. The Employee Retirement Income Security Act (ERISA) of 1974 requires defined benefit pension plans that offer an annuity as a payment option to provide a qualified joint-and-survivor annuity (QJSA) as the default benefit payment for married participants. A QJSA is an immediate annuity for the life of the participant and a survivor annuity for the life of the participant's spouse. The amount of the survivor annuity may not be less than 50 percent, or more than 100 percent, of the amount payable during the time the participant and spouse are both alive. The annuity payable for the life of the participant is lower than that for a straight life annuity; to account for the increased length of time over which payments will be made, this reduction may be a percentage of the straight life benefit, such as 10 percent, or may be based on the life expectancy of the participant and spouse.

Percentage of unreduced accrued benefit. Under this method, the participant's pension is not reduced to adjust for survivor benefits. The participant will receive an amount equal to the straight life annuity, and the spouse will receive a proportion of that amount, often 50 percent, should the participant die.

Lump-sum payment. The participant may opt for a full lump sum, with no further benefits received from the plan. If a plan provides for a partial lump-sum payment, the participant will receive a reduced annuity as well.

Defined Contribution Plans

Defined contribution plans are retirement plans that specify the level of employer contributions and place those contributions into individual employee accounts.

TYPES OF PLANS

Savings and thrift plans. Employees may contribute a predetermined portion of earnings (usually pretax)—all or part of which the employer matches—to an individual account. Employers may match a fixed percentage of employee contributions or a percentage that varies by length of service, amount of employee contribution, or other factors. Contributions are invested as directed by the employee or employer. Although usually designed as a long-term savings vehicle, savings-and-thrift plans may allow withdrawals and loans before retirement.

Deferred profit-sharing plans. In this type of defined contribution plan, a company credits shares of company profits to participating employees' accounts. Plans may set a fixed formula for sharing profits, but are not required to do so. Profit-sharing contributions to employees' accounts may be at the discretion of the company. Companies must set a method of allocating profit-sharing contributions to individual employees. Common allocation methods include allocation proportional to employee salary and equal allocation to all employees. Contributions and any accrued investment earnings on the accounts normally are not distributed until an employee's retirement from the company. The plan may allow employee contributions, but employees seldom are required to contribute to the plan.

Money purchase pension plans. Fixed employer contributions, typically calculated as a percentage of employee earnings, are allocated to individual employee accounts each year. Some plans may allow employee contributions, but employees usually are not required to make any contributions. Employers also may make profit-sharing contributions to these plans at their discretion.

Employee stock ownership plans (ESOPs). The employer pays a designated amount, often borrowed, into a fund that is then invested, primarily in company stock. Any debt incurred in the purchase of the stock is repaid by the company. Stock is then distributed to employees according to a formula.

Individual retirement accounts (IRAs). An IRA is a retirement savings plan. There are several types of IRAs: traditional IRAs, Roth IRAs, simplified employee pension (SEP) IRAs, and savings-incentive match plans for employees (SIMPLE) IRAs.

Traditional and Roth IRAs are established by individuals who are allowed to contribute earnings up to a set maximum dollar amount. SEPs and SIMPLE plans are retirement plans established by employers.

Simplified employee pensions (SEPs). An individual retirement account (IRA) is established for each eligible employee. The employee is immediately vested in employer contributions and generally directs the investment of the money.

Savings-incentive match plans for employees (SIMPLE) plan. This type of plan is limited to employers with fewer than 100 employees and who also do not have any other qualified retirement plan. SIMPLE plans can be either part of a 401(k) plan or established as IRAs. Employers must either make matching contributions of up to 3 percent of compensation or make a 2-percent non-elective contribution to all eligible employees. Participants who are 50 years or older may make additional pretax employee contributions into a SIMPLE plan.

METHODS OF CONTRIBUTIONS

Pre-tax contributions. This type of contribution is a feature of many savings-and-thrift plans and other defined contribution plans that allow employees to make contributions to deferred compensation plans through salary reduction agreements before federal and state taxes are deducted from pay. Distributions from a plan funded by pre-tax contributions are taxable at distribution.

Post-tax contributions. This type of contribution combines features of a Roth IRA plan and a 401(k) or

403(b) plan. Under these plans, employees are allowed to make part or all of their retirement plan contributions after taxes have been deducted, similar to the way a Roth IRA plan works. Post-tax contributions and their earnings are not subject to income tax upon distribution.

Amounts up to Internal Revenue Code (IRC) limit. The IRC provides for dollar limitations on benefits and contributions under qualified defined contribution plans.

INVESTMENT CHOICES

Company stock. Employees receive equity in the company that sponsors the defined contribution plan.

Common stock fund. This is a professionally managed fund invested in the common stock of a variety of companies.

Fixed-interest securities. These securities include bonds and other nonfederal instruments that pay a fixed interest rate over a predetermined period.

Diversified investments. These are professionally managed funds that are invested in more than one type of equity or debt instrument.

Money market fund. This is a professionally managed mutual fund that invests in short-term Treasury bills, certificates of deposit, or corporate bonds. The fund managers sell shares to investors, who receive regular payments of interest.

Life cycle fund. This is a balanced fund designed to become more conservative as the investor approaches retirement by moving from equity funds to fixed-income mutual funds.

WITHDRAWALS

Prior to normal payout (usually at retirement), defined contribution plan participants may be allowed to withdraw all or a portion of the employer funds from their accounts. Although most early withdrawals incur tax penalties, hardship withdrawals do not. To avoid tax penalties, many plans have loan provisions that allow employees to borrow from their accounts, with interest, for a specified period.

Hardship withdrawals. Employees usually are not penalized when money is withdrawn as a result of a hardship, often defined as the death or illness of a family member, educational expenses, sudden uninsured losses, or a need to prevent eviction from one's primary residence.

Loans. Defined contribution plans may allow participants to borrow employer funds, with interest, from their accounts. Loan amounts often are limited to a portion of the account balance. They usually have to be repaid within 5 years, but longer payment periods may apply for home purchase or renovation loans.

Transfers or rollovers. A rollover is a direct payment of plan benefits from a defined contribution plan into an IRA or another employer's plan. In a direct rollover, the employee is not taxed on the payment until it is withdrawn or distributed later.

Vesting

Vesting refers to the amount of time a participant must work before earning a nonforfeitable right to a retirement benefit. Once the participant is vested, the accrued benefit is retained even if the worker leaves the employer before reaching retirement age. Under ERISA, defined contribution plans are subject to the same vesting rules as defined benefit plans, but vesting schedules vary. Vesting schedules apply only to employer contributions; employee contributions (including pretax contributions) are always 100 percent vested.

Immediate full vesting. An employee is 100 percent vested immediately upon enrollment in the plan.

Cliff vesting. No vesting occurs until an employee satisfies the service requirements for 100-percent vesting—for example, 5 years.

Graded vesting. An employee's nonforfeitable percentage of employer contributions increases over time, until reaching 100 percent.

Employer Contribution Methods

Specified matching percent. This feature is common in savings-and-thrift plans. The employer matches a specified percentage of employee contributions. The matching percentage can vary by length of service, amount of employee contribution, and other factors.

Fixed percentage of profits formula. This feature is common in deferred profit sharing plans. The employer contributes a fixed percentage of total annual profits to the plan. For example, no matter what the level of profits, 5 percent is contributed to the plan. Profits may include those for the entire company or just those in a specific business unit. In a variation of this formula, employers set aside a reserve amount of profits (for example, $1 million) and pay only a fixed percentage of any profits above this amount into the employees' defined contribution plan.

Percentage of employee earnings. The employer contributes a fixed percentage of each employee's earnings to his or her individual account. This feature is common in money purchase plans.

RELATED PLANS AND TERMS

Stock bonus plan. Contributions are placed in a trust fund that invests in securities, including those of the employing company. This type of plan is financed by the employer or jointly by the employer and employee. Upon the employee's retirement or separation from the company, proceeds from the trust fund are paid out in the form of company stock or cash.

Automatic enrollment. As soon as eligibility requirements are met, employees become covered under a plan, but have the right to decline coverage at any time. A minimum default employee contribution and default investment vehicles usually are set, but employees may choose to contribute a different percentage and change investments.

Automatic escalation. Employee contributions are automatically increased at a predetermined rate over time, raising the contribution rate as a share of earnings. Employees may choose to contribute a different percentage.

Chart Data Sources

Figure 2: 2016 US Life Expectancy

New York State Department of Health
http://bit.ly/LifeET

Figure 3: Median US House Prices

United States Census Bureau
http://bit.ly/MedHouse

Figure 3: Inflation

US Inflation Calculator
http://bit.ly/InfRates

Figure 6: Years in Retirement by Birth Year

New York State Department of Health
http://bit.ly/LifeET

Figure 7: Retirement Income Sources

The Wall Street Journal
http://bit.ly/RINat

Figure 8: January 1 S&P 500 Value

Google.com/Finance
http://bit.ly/DailySP

Figure 9: Annual S&P 500 Gain and Loss

Google.com/Finance
http://bit.ly/DailySP

Index

Made in the USA
Monee, IL
04 November 2026

67380494R00079